D1545532

SEAWEED MEMORIES
IN THE JAWS OF THE SEA

HEINRICH BECKER was born in Germany in 1907. In 1934 he obtained a doctorate in folklore and wrote a book about the boatmen of the Elbe — his native people. He then became interested in Ireland's oral tradition and in 1938 he headed for Ireland to study Irish and Gaelic folklore. He spent seven months learning Irish at University College Galway, and for many years afterwards was a regular visitor to the Aran Islands and Connemara, where he perfected his Irish and collected folklore from the people. This book is a collection of many of the stories he gathered, almost sixty years ago, about seaweed and every aspect of the sea. *Seaweed Memories* also contains some of Heinrich Becker's photographs of the people of the west in the 1930s and 1940s, and of their precarious life in the jaws of the sea.

SEAWEED MEMORIES

IN THE JAWS OF THE SEA

HEINRICH BECKER

Seaweed stories and seaweed lore from Irish tradition:
translated from the editor's Irish collection
I mBéal na Farraige (Cló Iar-Chonnachta, 1997)

WOLFHOUND PRESS

First published in 2000
Wolfhound Press Ltd
68 Mountjoy Square
Dublin 1, Ireland

Tel: (353-1) 874 0354
Fax: (353-1) 872 0207

© 2000 Heinrich Becker

All rights reserved. No part of this book may be reproduced or utilised in any
form or by any means electronic, digital or mechanical including photography,
filming, video recording, photocopying, or by any information storage and
retrieval system or shall not, by way of trade or otherwise, be lent, resold or
otherwise circulated in any form of binding or cover other than that in which it
is published without prior permission in writing from the publisher.

The Arts Council
An Chomhairle Ealaíon
Wolfhound Press receives financial assistance from the Arts
Council/An Chomhairle Ealaíon, Dublin.

British Library Cataloguing in Publication Data
A catalogue record for this book is available from the British Library.

ISBN 0-86327-835-3

10 9 8 7 6 5 4 3 2 1

The photographs in this book are all from the author's private collection.

Cover photographs: Heinrich Becker
Cover Design: Graham Thew Design
Typesetting: Wolfhound Press
Printed in the Republic of Ireland by ColourBooks, Dublin

— Contents —

INTRODUCTION 11

STORYTELLING LONG AGO 15
Joe Ó Domhnaill

CHAPTER ONE:

THE STORIES 25
1 Wedged Between Two Rocks 25
Labhrás Ó Conghaile, Baile an Fhorma
2 'The Sea Took Me with Her in her Mouth' 26
Máirtín Seoighe, Baile an Fhorma, Inis Oírr
3 Rescued Drowning Man Breaks Taboo of Thanks 28
Val Ó Donnchadha, Bantrach Ard, Cill Chiaráin
4 Taboo of Saving Drowning People — 31
Feared and Observed
Micheál Ó Cearbhalláin, Carna
5 The Sea Caught Jamesy at Leic Dhubh 32
Cóilí Ó Conghaile, Baile Thiar, Inis Oírr
6 The Risk of Rowing in the Bow and its Remedy 33
Pádraig Ó Ceannabháin, Bantrach Ard, Cill Chiaráin
7 Val's Opinion on the Tying of the Legs 34
Val Ó Donnchadha, Bantrach Ard, Cill Chiaráin
8 There is a Peculiar Tide Tonight 35
Cóilín Ó Conghaile, Baile an Lurgain (Baile Thuas)
9 Trapped Foot Freed by Cutting Laces 36
Ciarán Mac an Iomaire, An Cuillín, Carna
10 Old Shoe as Mock Man-of-War (Song) 38
Seán Ó Conghaile, Cnoc na hAille, Indreabhán, Connemara
11 Slippery Strapweed Mound Causes Drowning 40
Pádraig Ó Loideáin, Maol Rua, Maoinis, Carna

12 Drowning due to Excessive Load   41
    Pádraig Ó Máille, Cor na Rón Láir, Cois Fharraige
13 *Climín* Drags Man off Pier   43
    Peadar Ó Ceannabháin, Cill Chiaráin
14 The Sham Seaweed Raft Drowns Man   44
    Aíne Ní Choisdealbha (Aged 12), National School,
    Ros a' Mhíl
15 Seaweed Raft, Crosspole, Inlet and Threshold   45
    Peadar Ó Ceannabháin, Carna
16 Making and Transport of Seaweed Raft
    and its Breaking up by Storm   46
    Peadar Ó Ceannabháin, Bantrach Ard, Cill Chiaráin
17 The Reason for the Name 'Na Foiriúin Bháite'   48
    Peadar Ó Ceannabháin, Cill Chiaráin
18 Origin of the Name 'Caladh na gClimíní'   49
    (Landing-place of the Seaweed-rafts)
    Val Ó Donnchadha, Bantrach Ard, Cill Chiaráin
19 *Creathnach*-Picking Girls on Rocky Islet Drowned by Tide   49
    Máirtín Ó Domhnaill, Baile Thiar, Inis Oírr
20 Taboo of Retrieving Corpse from Sea Observed   52
    Labhrás Ó Conghaile, Baile an Fhorma, Inis Oírr
21 Pregnant Girl to be Drowned on *Creathnach* Rock   53
    Val Ó Donnchadha, Bantrach Ard, Cill Chiaráin

CHAPTER TWO
Adventures and Wonder Stories   55
22 Diving to the Sea-bed to Release the Grapnel   55
    Val Ó Donnchadha, Bantrach Ard, Cill Chiaráin
23 Marcas Lifted Six Hundredweight of Kelp   56
    Val Ó Donnchadha, Bantrach Ard, Cill Chiaráin
24 Conroy Woman Shifts Stranded Boat, Carries Five   57
    Hundred and Fifty Pounds' Weight of Kelp
    Mícheál Mac an Iomaire, An Cuillín, Cill Chiaráin
25 Dog Takes Seaweed News Home   60
    Willy Ó Conghaile, Baile Thiar, Inis Oírr

— Contents —

26   Calemelassity: a New Word for *Coirleach* (strapweed)   62
Val Ó Donnchadha, Bantrach Ard, Cill Chiaráin

27   'Upon My Soul, We would Eat the Neap Tide Itself'   64
Pádraic Mac Donnchadha, Ros a' Mhíl

28   Astray in Fog   64
Seosamh Ó Flatharta, Baile an Chaisleáin, Inis Oírr

29   Porter and Songs instead of Burning Kelp   66
Peadar Seoighe, Baile an Fhorma, Inis Oírr

30   Don't Mind the Flies — They are Some of Your Ancestors   68
Peadar Seoighe, Baile an Fhorma, Inis Oírr

31   The Fight of the Two Master Burners   70
Peadar Seoighe, Baile an Fhorma, Inis Oírr

32   Selling Weed in Kinvara   73
Peadar Seoighe, Baile an Fhorma, Inis Oírr

33   Burning the Poor Widow's Kelp   75
Peadar Seoighe, Baile an Fhorma, Inis Oírr

34   Yarn about the Seaweed-rafts in Kinvara   79
Val Ó Donnchadha, Bantrach Ard, Cill Chiaráin

CHAPTER THREE
Gains and Losses   80
35   Kelp Thrown Overboard   80
Peadar Seoighe, Baile an Fhorma, Inis Oírr

36   Seaweed-laden *Púcán* Breaks in Two   81
Val Ó Donnchadha, Bantrach Ard, Cill Chiaráin

37   The Kelp-test Swindle   83
Máirtín Ó Domhnaill, Baile Thiar, Inis Oírr

CHAPTER FOUR
Discussions and Fighting   85
38   Fight with Seaweed Hook — Sea Takes Cut
Strapweed Out   85
Mairtin Seoighe, Baile an Fhorma, Inis Oírr

39   'Watch out for Johnny Rankel!'   87
Seán Ó Conghaile, Cnoc na hAille, Indreabhán

40 Tough Talk at Seaweed Boundary   88
    Ciarán Mac an Iomaire, An Cuillín, Cill Chiaráin
41 Jealous Man Strikes Strapwrack Cutter with Crosspole   89
    Val Ó Donnchadha, Bantrach Ard, Cill Chiaráin
42 Widow Attacks Seaweed Thieves with Stones   90
    Ciarán Mac an Iomaire, An Cuillín, Cill Chiaráin

CHAPTER FIVE
Law and the Courts   92
43 Court over Broken Jaw   92
    Micheál Mac an Iomaire, An Cuillín, Carna
44 The Judge Learns His Lesson   93
    Cóilín Ó Cualáin, Meall Rua, Maoinis, Carna
45 Seagulls and Sods   95
    Ciarán Mac an Iomaire, An Cuillín, Cill Chiaráin
46 No Map, No Proof   97
    Micheál Ó Cearbhaláin, Carna
47 Case on Rambling Weed Dismissed   98
    Val Ó Donnchadha, Bantrach Ard, Cill Chiaráin

CHAPTER SIX
Tricks and Theft   99
48 Thief, Beggar, Murderer   99
    Pádraig Ó Máille, Corr na Rón, Láir, Indreabhán
49 Laceweed Trickster Outwits Porter Trickster   101
    Cóilí, Ó Conghaile, Baile Thiar, Inis Oírr
50 The Stolen Seaweed Raft   102
    Micheál Ó Cearbhaláin, Carna
51 Keening Puts Greedy Seaweed Gatherer to Flight   103
    Pádraicín Ó Conghaile, Baile Thiar, Inis Oírr
52 'The Sheet Has Not Been Wetted Yet Beside Them'   104
    Seán Ó Conghaile, Cnoc na hAille, Indreabhán
53 Clever Servant Boy Tricks Greedy Master   105
    Pádraig Mac Donnchada, Ros na Mhíl
54 Two Lobsters as Bribe (Kelp Test)   107
    Val Ó Donnchadha, Bantrach Ard, Cill Chiaráin

— *Contents* —

CHAPTER SEVEN
The Living Dead and The Fairy Host   109
55   Dead Sailor's Thanks for Burial   109
Val Ó Donnchadha, Bantrach Ard, Cill Chiaráin
56   Dead Woman Assists Seaweed Gatherer   110
Val Ó Donnchadha, Bantrach Ard, Cill Chiaráin
57   Spirit Advises against Seaweed Theft   112
Cóilín Ó Cualáin, Meall Rua, Maoinis, Carna
58   The Fairies Punish Nocturnal Seaweed Gatherer   113
Seán Ó Conghaile, Scoil Náisiúnta, Inis Meáin
59   Sabbath Seaweed Gatherers Penalised by Ghostly Beings   114
Pheadaí Ó Conghaile, Baile an Chaisleáin, Inis Oírr
60   Ghostboat Appears After Seaweed Theft   116
Val Ó Donnchadha, Bantrach Ard, Cill Chiaráin
61   Fairies Fighting during Kelp Burning   118
Cóilí, Ó Conghaile, Baile Thuas, Inis Oírr
62   Fairies Gathering Seaweed at Sunset   120
Máirtín Seoighe, Baile an Fhorma, Inis Oírr
63   Seaweed Sprite Diverts Fairies   121
Val Ó Donnchadha, Bantrach Ard, Cill Chiaráin
64   Girl Dances to Fairy Music and is Spirited away   123
Seán de Bhailís, Sruthán, Inis Mór

CHAPTER EIGHT
About Demons and Devils   124
65   Big Walsh Kills Ghost with Black-handled Knife   124
Val Ó Donnchadha, Bantrach Ard, Cill Chiaráin
66   Storm-witches Try to Drown Big Walsh   127
Val Ó Donnchadha, Bantrach Ard, Cill Chiaráin
67   Cursing the Gale Saves Seaweed Boat   129
Peadar Seoighe, Baile an Fhorma, Inis Oírr
68   Black Merman Tries to Board Boat   131
Val Ó Donnchadha, Bantrach Ard, Cill Chiaráin
69   Seaweeder Sees Mermaid   132
Seósamh Ó Flatharta, Baile an Chaisleán, Inis Oírr

CHAPTER NINE
Work Taboos and Other Wonder Stories 135
70 Holy Water Sends the Redweed Ashore 135
   Val Ó Donnchadha, Bantrach Ard, Cill Chiaráin
71 Horse Breaks Knee of May-Day Seaweed-Gatherer 137
   Máirtín Seoighe, Baile an Fhorma, Inis Oírr
72 The Sea Takes the Seaweed of St Stephen's Day 138
   Val Ó Donnchadha, Bantrach Ard, Cill Chiaráin
73 The Sea Takes Sunday Seaweed 139
   Máirtín Ó Domhnaill, Baile Thiar, Inis Oírr
74 Sunday's Seaweed without Crop 140
   Labhrás Ó Conghaile, Baile an Fhorma, Inis Oírr
75 Instructive Revelation on Sunday Work 141
   Labhrás agus Máirtín Ó Conghaile, Baile an Fhorma, Inis Oírr
76 Christmas Seaweed Did Not Rot 142
   Val Ó Donnchadha, Bantrach Ard, Cill Chiaráin
77 Seal as Omen of Dry Weather 143
   Peadar Seoige, Baile an Fhorma, Inis Oírr
78 Seal Prevents Seaweeders from Working 145
   Pádraic Ó Máille, Cor na Rón Láir, Indreabhan
79 Broken Taboo of Silence Impedes Fern Cure 146
   Peadar Seoighe, Baile an Fhorma, Inis Oírr
80 Curing Skin Disease by Bladderwrack 148
   Mícheál Ó Donnchada, Baile Thiar, Inis Oírr
81 Sea Urchins' Spikes Can be Removed with the Ebb Tide 149
   Peadar Seoige, Baile an Fhorma, Inis Oírr
82 The Secret of the Danes' Fertiliser 151
   Labhrás Ó Conghaile, Baile an Fhorma, Inis Oírr
83 Refuge for Tailor from Bull on Seaweed Cock 153
   Seósamh Ó Flatharta, Baile an Chaisleán, Inis Oírr
84 Dog Kills Wild Cat 154
   Labhrás Ó Conghaile, Baile an Fhorma, Inis Oírr
85 Bream: Half Fish, Half Seaweed 157
   Ciarán Mac an Iomaire, An Cuillín, Cill Chiaráin
86 The Islanders' Way of Living 158
   Mícheál Ó Meachair, Baile an Chaisleáin, Inis Oírr

— Introduction —

This volume is a translation of *I mBéal na Farraige* (Cló Iar-Chonnachta, 1997), a collection of seaweed stories and seaweed lore from Irish tradition. All the material in that book was collected by me from the narration of Irish-speaking informants in the West of Ireland. It is now sixty years since I first became actively involved in collecting folklore in Irish about the sea, and all connected with it. I was introduced to Séamus Ó Duilearga in 1935 when he was on a lecture tour of Germany. He spent a few days in Marburg University where I was a lecturer in the Department of English. I had, by that time, finished my doctorate on folklore and had published a book on the oral traditions of the Elbe boatmen, being one of them myself by birth. I was fascinated by Ó Duilearga's account of the state of Irish folklore at that time and, as I understood from him that there was still a rich harvest to reap in the field of maritime folklore, I decided to come to Ireland.

I arrived in Ireland in 1938 and spent some seven months in University College, Galway, learning Irish and teaching German. I commenced collecting folklore in 1939 from school children in Rosaveel National School, with the assistance of Pádraig Ó hÉidhin, N.T. This material, along with all the material I have since collected, is in my private archive in Düren. It was a great pleasure to meet so many of the past pupils of this school, as well as so many other old friends at **Dúchas an Iarthair — Das Erbe des Westens**, an exhibition of my paintings that took place in UCG in 1995 to coincide with that institute's 150th Anniversary.

I spent the War years in Ireland as I was unable to return to live in Germany until 1952. Since then I have returned frequently to Ireland, collecting folklore and indulging in my other great passion, painting. Most of the tales in this book are memoirs, more or less realistic accounts of events that happened to the narrators or their acquaintances. They were collected in the Aran Islands and in Connemara and deal with all aspects of seaweed collecting. The seaweed industry is a very old one in Ireland. It is mentioned in the Old Irish laws (P. W. Joyce, *A Social History of Ancient Ireland*, Vol. 2, London 1903, 153-4; F. Kelly, *A Guide to Early Irish Law*, Dublin 1988, 107-8) and the excerpt from the 'Life of Senán' in the addendum to tale No. 19 illustrates the deadly dangers for those who were obliged to eke out a living from this kind of work.

The second narrative in this collection, 'The sea took me with her in her mouth', suggested the book's Irish title. It is a stark account of how the narrator escaped death from the jaws of the sea. The dangers and the hardships of life on the Atlantic coast of the West of Ireland in former times permeate these tales. Those who formed the original audience for these stories would have been reminded by them of the constant anger of the jealous and hungry sea. Although the industrial harvesting of seaweed is still carried on in the West of Ireland, these tales are for us a social document, a reminder of a type of life now almost vanished.

It has been swallowed up by the tidal wave of the modern world.

All the tales were told in Irish and now appear for the first time in English garb. As I have been engaged on this work for a number of years, various people have assisted me in the interpretation of the material at different stages of the work. The temptation to arrive at false interpretations of difficulties in the text, without the help of the local tradition-bearers, should not be underestimated, but should be avoided at all costs. Knowledge of local or regional expressions is of paramount importance. Nor should the help of local people in the unravelling of some of the more obscure passages in these texts be underestimated. An extreme example is the case of Labhrás Ó Conghaile, where he sometimes doesn't bother to finish a sentence in well-known stories, as he knew that the locals would know what he meant. The assistance of local people in this situation is invaluable. So as to avoid blunders, all queries were directed at the local people. I would like to extend my thanks, firstly, to the storytellers of course, without whom this book would never have been. They were always prepared to answer all my questions, repeat stories for me and to be of every assistance in my work. Thanks also to Pádraig, Micil Antoine, Éinne, Willy, Joseph Pháraicín, Tom, Aindí, Nóra, Mairéad, Máire and many others. Thanks also to Arndt Wigger, Wuppertal University and Die Deutsche Forschungsgemeinschaft for assistance rendered.

The editing of *I mBéal na Farraige* took place during prolonged stays in Áras na Gaeilge, National University of Ireland, Galway, in 1996 and 1997 when much of the final work on the translations in this volume was also accomplished. I wish to thank all those in NUIG who assisted me in this task, especially Feargal Ó Béarra. Máirtín Ó Briain gave me much invaluable assistance and encouragement. I also wish to thank Mícheál Ó Conghaile and Cló Iar-Chonnachta who published the original Irish language texts of *I mBéal na Farraige* and for all their work on that book, and Wolfhound Press for granting them the rights to do so.

HEINRICH BECKER,
Düren, August, 1998

— Storytelling Long Ago —

JOE Ó DOMHNAILL, INIS OÍRR

Visiting started around November, when the harvesting was finished — the wheat and the grain and the straw — when the houses were thatched and prepared for the winter. It was the custom of some of the people to visit neighbours whom they liked in their home and spend some of the nights with them. They would often go outside the village with the intention of visiting these people. It did not matter if the men were married or single, it was the custom to make these visits.

The girls would not leave their own home at night, it was not their habit. They stayed at home working, knitting, sewing, spinning, mending and making clothes, clothes for the household. Therefore, their mothers watched them every night. It was not their custom to go visiting, to go on the roads. Years ago the young girls made lace, earning money, and they continued with it at home at night. It was not the custom for married women to go visiting. They preferred to stay at home, in the house, teaching the children to do this kind of work.

Some people would begin to arrive at any time after supper (that is from seven), and it would not be long before a company of up to a dozen neighbours would be around the fire. After a short while talking about current affairs and the day's work somebody would ask the householder: 'Please tell a story.' The storyteller would answer: 'What kind of tale would you prefer?'

It was the enjoyment of listening to the householder, or to the storyteller who frequented the place, that drew people to the specific house, although the young men would also enjoy visiting there because of the young women in the house. But generally it was the fine tales told by the storyteller that mainly drew people there.

According as people began to arrive, the householder and the lady of the house welcomed them and a place was found for them beside the fire. Everybody who would visit would be welcomed, as was everybody who visited.

It was a matter of enjoyment for the people of the house that the visitors came, and if they did not come, if it happened that they stopped coming, they would be very surprised and would worry that they had done or said something that they did not like, something that had kept them away. And when they met them the following day they would ask them why they did not visit the house the previous night and to be certain to come that night, that they would like them to come.

They would discuss the current affairs and the past day's work and the work to be done the following day. There are many things, on sea and land, to discuss.

'I believe,' says the householder to one of the men, 'that you had a worrying day today landing the currach. 'Oh! yes,' says Seán. 'When we were half way in the Sound a heavy shower came and the sky darkened. The sea became rough and we had our job cut out to protect the currach from the sea. We encountered a rough sea in spite of our endeavours. It bore down on us, on the prow of the currach, and turned the currach windward. We would have been in danger of sinking if another wave followed it, because the currach would fill up with water.'

'But another wave did not come and we bailed out the currach. Nevertheless, it took us a long time to arrive, and the day was getting worse when we arrived at the end of the harbour. The sea was breaking on the harbour and we had to wait a long time to run the currach ashore. But we got the chance at last and we came ashore without anything happening to us. But mark my word, we were a tired, exhausted crew when we were home.'

'True for you, I understand well,' said the householder. 'Séamas,' the householder would say to another man, 'What kind of work were you engaged in today?'

'What I was doing today,' Séamas would say, 'was to try and free a horse from a fissure.'

'Séamas,' said the householder, a man from Forma, 'I believe that you had a hard job last night trying to free Joyce's horse from a fissure.'

'Yes,' said Séamas. 'The night was very bad on account of how dark it was. Indeed it was,' said Séamas. 'When I was going along the road, going to milk the cattle, the cows, when I looked over at the well, I saw Joyce's horse on the crag with its right foot stuck in a fissure. I put the can down and I ran over to the horse. I took off my belt and I tried to keep it calm. I did not see anybody passing by who could notify Joyce and I stayed by the horse's head for a good while. Finally, I saw a woman walking on the road and I shouted to her and told her to run down to the village and tell Joyce that the horse's foot was stuck in a fissure beside Iolán's well and to tell him to bring helpers with him along with crowbars, a sledge-hammer, and wedges. That woman was Margaret Flaherty and she went and gave them the news. A short while later they arrived, and began to break the stones on all sides of the fissure.'

'It was dark and raining heavily at this time and it was necessary to send someone to the village to fetch a lantern in order that we might have light.'

'More people came then and after a while there were many people around the horse. Some of them were holding the horse trying to keep it calm because it was agitated and it was in danger of killing itself.'

'It was twelve o' clock in the night when we freed her from the fissure. It appeared to us that she was not badly injured, just a few scratches on her leg. But I suspect that horse will do no heavy work for a long while.'

And in that manner accidents that happened at different times in the past are discussed. Things like that happen often in the island and there are enough of them to describe when they gather together at night.

And almost invariably there are people in the company who have spent much of the life on the mainland, or in England, or in America, or in Australia, or in the Indies: soldiers who have returned home from armies of other nations, sailors who have spent long periods sailing the sea, and who would describe the exotic lands and who have powerful thrilling tales about their exploits.

The householder and his wife were always very satisfied with that conversation because they enjoyed to hear those things and especially the things the people who had been abroad described. The young people in the company also liked it because they expected sooner or later to venture out in the world in the same way, and they wanted to find out from those people about the world outside.

Those are the matters they discuss every night and, as a consequence, the inhabitants of this island are well informed of the ways and affairs of the world, far wiser than visitors who come among them would imagine.

Later, when the children have been put to bed, the others would draw closer to the fire. The householder would fill his pipe and would settle down in the corner and the woman of the house would settle down in the opposite corner. When he had lit and smoked the pipe, one of the company would ask the householder:

'Please tell us a story, Máirtín.'

'What type of story would you like?' he would say, 'a story about the old times?' And he would tell a story then.

They were very keen to find out about the living conditions of the people in Ireland long ago, and about the fights between certain heroes described in the stories. And also about all the trouble, hardship, difficulty and injury the hero would suffer to rescue the young princess from the danger she was in, and all the combats he would have to fight against other heroes. There were, perhaps, heroes who had been enchanted by magicians.

Most of the stories dealt about the era of the Fianna and most of them were about Fionn mac Cumhaill and his heroes. Those men were capable of great actions and could endure any injury they received from combat with heroes who fought against them, and that is the subject matter, and the reason, that the people liked to hear the old stories from time to time. The storyteller never tired of telling these stories from year to year.

Many tales that did not involve the Fianna nor the Fenian era were also told, some about heroes who travelled to the Eastern World because they heard that there were mighty heroes there and they wished to compete against them in every sport on the playing field.

The stories, for instance, about Cearrbhach na Craoibhe. The Cearrbhach, the owner of the hound, travelled through many nations and he knew many places throughout the world, especially the countries of the East and the customs of the people there. Therefore, he could inform people who were headed to those countries.

The hero had to cross the sea to go to the Eastern World and he had to spend much time in preparing his ship. It often happened that a great storm would rise and the vessel would sink. Then he would have to swim until he came to the nearest land.

These things happened in some of the tales. There was an island on the way and generally it was near that island that the vessel would encounter the storm and the high seas and the strong currents. And when the crew of the vessel would swim to the island, it was found to be inhabited by evil people. A giant used to kill the people who came ashore. The hero would have to fight with the giant.

My grandfather knew two hundred stories. Fifty of them were about the Fianna of Ireland, stories about Fionn mac Cumhaill, Goll mac Mórna, Diarmaid ó Duibhne, Oscar and Oisín and Dearg Mór, the Great Hag and so on, Diarmaid and Gráinne, the Great Magic Hag, stories about the Hero with the Shining Sword, the Hero with the Short Sword, the Hero with the Sword of Light, stories about the Ogre of the Feats, the Hero from Greece and the wrestling with the Black Turk, stories about the Son of the King of Ireland, the Son of the King of Scandinavia, the Queen of the Eerie Island and many stories about the Black Thief.

He also told stories about the Gobán Saor, and Seáinín of the Little Bull and the Cat of the Cave.

'Have you ever heard the story about the Queen of the Eerie Island', he would say.

'No,' they would say.

The lady of the house and her daughter would speak. 'Oh, tell that story because it is a nice story.' And he would begin.

And then he would place his pipe near the hearth and would start the story like this.

'Once upon a time, a long time ago. If I were alive then I would not be so now, I would have an old story or a new story, or I would have no story...'

'There was a king's son....'

In order to narrate the story properly in the manner the storyteller was accustomed to, he should concentrate on the story he is telling. Therefore, he can do nothing else while telling the tale. He would stop at a certain point in the story if he wanted to smoke the pipe, to smoke tobacco. If the story were long he would stop at a certain point after a wondrous event had occurred in the tale, for example when two heroes who were engaged in combat and one of them had been defeated.

That would give him a chance to rest and to draw his breath. During that time the company would discuss the events narrated in the story up to that point.

They would praise the storyteller and the valorous deeds of the heroes until the tale was recommenced. During that time he would smoke his pipe while listening to them and their conversation. When he had smoked the pipe, he would set it aside, the talk would stop and everybody would be silent until he recommenced the tale. Then he would say:

'I am going to continue the story. Where did I stop?' He would be told. 'Oh, yes,' he would say and then he would continue.

If the tale were too long to finish that night he would say:

'Friends, I think that we will stop now, that we will call a halt now because it is time to go to bed. The story won't be finished tonight. Come back tomorrow night and I will tell you the rest of the story.'

'All right,' the company replied.

They would arise, one by one.

'All right,' everybody would say . 'Thank you and long life to you. That much of the story was fine. You told it well. It could not have been told better and we will not be satisfied until we hear the rest of the story.'

Everybody would arise. They would say: 'Good night to you.' And they would depart.

On the following day, other people would hear that he was telling the story and that night there would be extra people in the house listening to the story.

They would praise the storyteller again when the tale was finished and thank him and the housewife for the good fire and the heat during the two nights. The story-teller would answer them.

'I am proud that you liked the story so much, because I could see from the attention, from the silence you gave me and from the extra people who came here tonight that you were very interested in my story and the way I told it.'

'Oh, indeed!' they said, 'you told it very well. No story-teller could tell it better.' The following day, after we had lain in bed, the night after such a story, we would think about the heroes and the strong folk mentioned in the story. We would like to be as strong as them so that we could do those deeds.

We would gather together in the evening on the beach and we would be engaged in throwing stones and wrestling and the high-jump and running. We would fence one another.

The swords we had were long sticks with sharp points, about the length of a sword.

We would parry and thrust, but not strike a blow on one another, nor would we injure one another. If the sharp point that was on one man's stick touched the other man, that was a winning point and it would be reckoned that he had won, that that man had won.

Among the causes for the abandonment of stories is the First World War. So many wondrous things happened every day during the war. Another reason, there was no light, nor oil, nor candles for lighting in the houses and even if they were available it was illegal to light a light (to show a light) after nightfall.

People were not supposed to leave their home after nightfall. That finished off visiting and also storytelling. The old people were gradually dying. The young people did not maintain the stories and many stories, or most of them, were lost when the old people died.

Although most of the old storytellers have passed away, there are still people here who are able to tell many old stories if asked to do so. Some old stories are still told in a few houses, or on boats to spend the time, or on the road when people are working together repairing walls or work of that kind.

Because storybooks like Grimms' were circulating in recent years some of those stories have been mixed up with the old Irish stories and that has spoilt the stories. I have often recognised those stories because I had read them before that in Grimms' book.

— Chapter One —

THE STORIES

1

Wedged Between Two Rocks
Labhrás Ó Conghaile, Baile an Fhorma

We were there and we were collecting that seaweed. Myself and two other men, Micheál and Stiofán Ó Flaithearta were one day at the shore at Leic Trá Caorach, gathering seaweed to fertilise the potatoes. We had a large amount of the weed gathered, which was a day's work, and we filled a heavy load onto the donkey which he himself had and the two of us kept assisting the donkey until we reached the proper road from the strand.

We left the other man down below working at the seaweed. When we looked behind us as we were almost up, we saw a large wave coming. We could do nothing else but stay where we were and hold on to the donkey as best we could. The sea went as high as our shoulders, but with God's help, we were not knocked down and it subsided again. We kept our weight down on the donkey until the sea was gone, and we threw the load off him then and went for the other man then, Stiofán, and we were very much afraid thinking that we would never see him again.

We were looking and searching and we came upon him with his head in under a stone, covered with the sand and seaweed, his mouth and ears and every part of him full of it and he was unconscious. We cleaned him and we brought him up into the fresh breeze, and we were cleaning him until he began to gain consciousness. He said to us when the wave came that it lifted him like a small piece of wood, that it swept him up on to the top of the storm beach and that it brought him down again till he was half way when he happened to go down between these two large stones with the backwash. And the seaweed covered him then and the sand and the weight kept him there. That was what he had to tell us when he became conscious.

2 'The Sea Took Me with Her in her Mouth'
Máirtín Seoighe, Baile an Fhorma, Inis Oírr
(Account of seaweed work)

I was here one night and as I was, I went down to the shore to put up some seaweed ... gathering seaweed at Geata an tSolais — out at the lighthouse. We were gathering and there were two people from the village with us and, by dad,, we were gathering it up and there was a lot of seaweed on the foreshore. And, by dad, we weren't long gathering ... it wasn't long after that when the tide began to cover the seaweed we had gathered. And as it was, the four of us were beside one another gathering the seaweed and in the end we begrudged each other.

This breaker began to come in from the sea which we had always seen and the night was dark enough. And as it was, this breaker caught me and pulled me out in her mouth. And by dad, when she did, she brought me up for about a hundred and fifty yards on the top of the storm beach.

When the others looked there was no trace of me. They began searching for me, over and back in the seaweed. I could not be found and, by dad, when I couldn't, they didn't know where I was. The sea had taken my consciousness. But shortly afterwards I was found stretched out, up on the storm beach, covered in seaweed.

When he found me, he took me out, that's when I regained consciousness. I sat down on a pile of stones. And this breaker was going up on the storm beach. They carried me up to the road and I sat down there for about half an hour.

And when it was, then, we went down again to the seaweed, the four of us, gathering in the tide again. We thought it was ebbing but it was actually flooding. So we started gathering again. And we gathered ... oh a big pile of seaweed each, for two hours. It was two o'clock in the night that time — the deadly time of night.

We were there and had that much seaweed piled up, each of us had around two hundred baskets of winter seaweed gathered. It was rods at that time of year, in October.

That was all right, I stood up and took the basket and put the sheepskin on me. And the man who was on the other side of me, took his basket and put his sheepskin on him. When we went up with the baskets, on the way down this great breaker came and didn't leave a sop of seaweed that she didn't sweep away with her.

And we found no trace of any bit of seaweed that night. We sat up on the storm shore and were fed up enough with ourselves, that we had no seaweed at all to put in the basket and us dead out and tired.

'We might as well go home for a drop of tea.' And we did. We got in home and we drank the tea. And we went out, over the road again to Cloch Chormaic. There was a great amount of seaweed there — *searod* — when we went over.

We started filling. We took off our shoes and were saving weed till day came. And that was the time the people were starting to come in the morning. And we longed for a drop of tea. We came in and put down the tea and drank it. And we went out again and we were there till the sun sank in the ground.

The whole village, by that time were down on the shore and the stone walls were covered with seaweed. We were going, about a quarter of a mile with our baskets, in the end. The place was full, in front of us but at the end of the day we were exhausted and dead out, when we came home at half past ten at night. And I tell you we were tired that night.

3 Rescued Drowning Man Breaks Taboo of Thanks
Val Ó Donnchadha, Bantrach Ard, Cill Chiaráin

I often heard around here in Connemara, whether it is true or not, that it was said that any man saved from drowning, never expressed thanks to any man. You would think it a strange thing. But I know one man who thanked my father himself and his two comrades, whom they saved from drowning. That is a man from Coill Sáile, Tomás Phaitseach a' Griallais.

He and children and young men and women were picking *creathnach* on Eagle Rock. He was on the north side, where I was telling you a short while ago, and it is still said by old fishermen that no breaker ever came in there, but that the sea breaks out from the land. It is called Maidhm Leac Dhearg [the Wave of the Red Rock].

But Curran or Paitseach, the Grealish man, was up there and the retreating wave took him out. The women were inside and they were shouting at these fishermen and they were a good bit out lifting lobster pots. They moved in and he was there — he was an old man at that time. The place was very rough — a tossed sea. Five or six perhaps or a dozen often, when they would get a fine day and a calm sea, perhaps they could pick on that day half the year's supply of *creathnach*, picking it when the tide was out. It was called *creathnach dhiúilicíneach* [*creathnach* with mussels growing on it]. It is good when dried in the sun. It is very good for the winter, for sauce and it is said that it is healthy.

Anyhow they were picking, but Tomás went too far down and he was carried out by the retreating wave. But they did not see him. But the women were inside and the children and they were screaming. But someone in the boat said that there must be someone in danger of drowning. And they [the fishermen] moved in and Tomás Phaitseach was out in the wave, sitting down in the sea and going in and out with the tossed sea and his hair spread out on top of the water. They did their best to save him. They went out and they let down the mooring stone as far as the mooring rope allowed them and they moved inland and they took him out of the water.

They went south then to the harbour, Eagle Rock harbour, a quiet place and they put him ashore on the mainland. The poor man was put lying on his stomach (mouth underneath) and they were saying that a whole barrel of seawater came out of his mouth. He was not regaining consciousness. He must have been near enough to death when he was picked up. Someone said, 'If there was someone who could put a bit of tobacco in his mouth, if there was any vein at all alive in his heart that he would pull through. But Curran was never without tobacco, so he put his hand in his pocket and took a good slice of tobacco from a piece that he had, and he was trying to put it under his back teeth. You often heard of the drowning man's grip; his teeth were so tight that you wouldn't open them with a pincers. Whatever way he put his thumb in, when Tomás got a hold of it, he bit on it and almost made two halves of it.

'Ah,' said Curran, 'old debts.' Curran used have a saying always which they used to repeat. I saw him, Curran, God rest his soul, I barely remember him. He used to have a saying in which he said, 'as the beggar said.' 'As the beggar said,' said Curran, 'I had nothing from it except the loss of my thumb.' He saved his thumb the day the drowning man bit on it. He saved it, but it was sore. But as I was saying to you before, that no one ever thanked anyone, or so it is said, for saving him from danger of drowning. But poor Tomás was not like that. In the first public house in which he met my father or the men who were with him, he thanked them a lot, and he was very grateful to them.

But I suppose he was not fated to die because it was said there was a priest in the place one time, and that he was looking for a passage across the bay. The day was very windy, north west storm. He found no man in his travels who said he would take him to Leitir Caladh but Tomás's father, Paitseach a' Ghriallais. He was a young man at that time and he went across in his púcán boat with him and he left him over there.

'Muise,' said the priest when he went out, 'may God spare you your life and your health, and I hope to God that no one of your descendants will ever be drowned or thrown into the sea.'

And it is said that no man of the Grealishes was ever drowned since.

4 Taboo of Saving Drowning People Feared and Observed
Micheál Ó Cearbhalláin, Carna

As I heard it, about thirty years ago, that is about 1940 or maybe 1938 in Cill Chiaráin, the race day was on, a regatta, and there was one race and there were at least two gleoiteogs or maybe three in the race. They had to go to buoys and back again.

Well, the first time that they were passing the buoys, the first gleoiteog was slightly ahead. He went around the buoy. He might have gone a bit too hasty and he capsized in the water. In those gleoiteogs there were at least two people in each one. One of the two attempted to catch on to the second gleoiteog which was near him. He put his hand up on the gunnel of the boat, up around the boat. The next thing, on the second boat there was a man, there were a few and one of them picked up an axe and he chopped all his fingers off the lad who was trying to get into the boat. Now I didn't hear if that lad died, but anyhow he didn't get a chance to get into the second boat. And then the second boat finished and won the race.

The essence of this story is that many of the people in Connemara, even today, believe that it isn't right to save a person from drowning. It is right to save them anywhere else, but not from drowning. If they save them from drowning they believe that they themselves will lose their lives at some point in the water. They think that there is a space for everyone in the water and that if it is not filled with the corpse of a person, [that is to say] the person who is destined to go there, the sea must put another person in that place. And usually it is the person who saves [another] person who enters that place. That is the type of belief which prevails among many people in Connemara.

Question: Where did you hear that story?

Answer: I heard this story from one of the lads who works in the factory, after a little spot of trouble which I had myself the day of the races. We have had races here now for five years or more. It happened that when we were presenting the prizes, up to eight people came up on the stage. I myself nearly got hit, but I was able to make a good retreat and made no bad stand. I went into the office and but for that I myself maybe would have been beaten up. And after that, one of the lads from the factory told me about what had happened about thirty years ago with the races. He said that it is very difficult to run such events now in Cill Chiaráin because there isn't much sportsmanship there at all. It's a great pity. People go out and if they don't win they aren't prepared to participate in the races at all.

5 The Sea Caught Jamesy at Leic Dhubh (Black Rock)
Cóilí Ó Conghaile, Baile Thiar, Inis Oírr

Jamesy up here, he was an old man, and he went out picking creathnach. And when he did, there was a big sea running. Of course, his wife thought that he was as sensible as an old cat, and that there was no danger that the sea would catch him unawares. But, as you say, he turned his back on the sea, his back, and he was picking the creathnach until this sea came from the west. Out on Leac Dhubh the sea runs for a quarter of a mile almost on the shallow shelf there.

Jamesy did not feel anything until the wave hit him. He had a hold of the basket in which he had the *creathnach*. There was a shoulder strap on it and he had a hold of the basket. The sea hit him and it lifted him and the basket clean off the ground. He let the basket go. He was thrown up the shore further and like the other man, he managed to get a hold of a stone, and if he did itself, it was with a drowning man's grip.

The sea began to retreat again and he kept his grip. And the sea retreated a quarter of a mile again so that the place was dry again. But when he looked around him he had nothing left to him. The basket was halfway over to the lighthouse, drifting on top of the water and the *creathnach* in it. He had nothing coming home. The sea took the *creathnach* from him, and he was lucky he wasn't gone himself.

'Ah muise,' said his wife when he arrived home, 'I thought you had some sense. If it was a small young child', she said, 'that had gone out and had that much happen to him, he would be blamed. But you who were as wise as an old cat, you got caught by the sea.'

6 **The Risk of Rowing in the Bow and its Remedy**
Pádraig Ó Ceannabháin, Bantrach Ard, Cill Chiaráin

I don't know what was wrong with himself.

'Paddy,' says he, 'I don't feel as good today as I used to, but would you have the spunk to row in the bow?'

'I'll go indeed, Réamonn,' says I.

'But look it here,' says he, 'You might break a rowing pin,' says he. 'God bless you,' says he, 'you're fine and fit,' says he. 'I see you rowing wilder than myself. But see now, I will tie your legs,' says he, 'your two legs and if even you break a rowing pin,' says he, 'you won't go overboard.'

But I was telling the story one time over in Ros Muc, one day in Tí Mhaidhceo, it was a pub. A small, old Munsterman was there. Himself and another man were in there. 'Well,' says he, 'that's the first time that I heard of a man tying his legs,' says he, 'in a boat.'

7 Val's Opinion on the Tying of the Legs
Val Ó Donnchadha, Bantrach Ard, Cill Chiaráin

Right enough there was Pádraig and his father, God rest his soul, and Réamon Mac Donnchadha, whom he was talking about. He came up to this village from Inis Mhic Cionnaith, in Carraroe. He had no experience with a púcán boat but he knew about hookers and big boats and of course he was very skilled in handling the canvas currach. I saw him working in it and I myself was out at sea with him taking in [lobster] pots. But I never saw nor heard him saying that (i.e. the feet being tied).

But the man I was telling you about now — I thought it a strange thing for him to be saying to a stranger that he would tie any man's feet that was going to row in the bow of a boat. God save us, no man with a spark of sense in his head would do that, because if the thole-pin let you down or if your oars failed, you would be drowned and dead outright.

But if you keep your feet free, you have some sort of chance. Often, I myself was out rowing in the bow, on a bad day and I wouldn't let anyone tie my feet. You can safely say that I wouldn't allow it, or my brothers either.

But people are always saying things, with all due respect to the company, excuse me, that neither have head nor tail to them.

8 There is a Peculiar Tide Tonight
*Cóilín Ó Conghaile, Baile an Lurgain
(Baile Thuas)*

One night we went back collecting seaweed and the sign we had was, when the tide would start going out, that the ebb tide would turn when the moon would rise. Because when the moon starts to wane, it won't rise, but will only rise with the ebb tide. But we were waiting until we saw the moon rising. And off we went, back as far as Áit an Chuain, where the seaweed was. And we were not long there, just down, gathering, when another man came up beside us. And we were all making a big cock, throwing [seaweed] up, up.

And, by dad, later when he thought it was ebbing, it was actually flooding, and the big heap that we had made — the sea came and put it seven yards up above where it was. I said that I thought it would be ebbing when the moon would rise.

'I thought so myself,' said the other man, 'but it is actually flooding tonight, as we should not have come for another while.'

But we were gathering and when we thought it was at half-ebb, the tide was as high as ever. And I can tell you that we were wet. And then a breaker came and we were trying to keep it [the seaweed] against the sea. The sea came and lifted the heap and ourselves, and we were covered in seaweed. We barely had our heads above water, trying to keep the water out of our mouths. But we got away.

'Well,' we said to one another, 'it is a strange kind of tide we have tonight. Instead of ebbing it is flooding'. But that is the rout ... the sea never went higher after that. But indeed, we were wet and very wet. And then when the seaweed was gathered and collected we went home, and put on dry clothes, and waited until it was day, and we went back and started to bring it up [above the high water mark]. And that is the small story I had.

Yes, the sea is always hungry, because a lot of people are always perishing in it. She will take all she gets, all that happens. If death is their destiny, they will be drowned. And there is many a person that survives, if he goes up on a plank in the sea, he may survive or something else may take him. But hundreds are being drowned. Don't turn your back to the sea, because you don't know how far in she is going to come.

9 Trapped Foot Freed by Cutting Laces
Ciarán Mac an Iomaire, An Cuillín, Carna

My grandfather and his brother and a neighbour went out once to Carraig an Mhatail cutting seaweed. They almost had the boat laden when the foot of one of the men got stuck, and it was failing them in every way to pull it out of the fissure.

The tide was coming in and the water was rising on him, and he said to cut off his foot with the sickle before he drowned. But one of the other men had the idea that if he loosened the lace or if he cut it that the foot would come out of the shoe. They cut the lace and the foot came up freely. He was saved without cutting off his foot with a sickle.

Question: How many miles out was it?

Answer: This rock is about six or seven miles or perhaps eight miles from the mainland. It's out in the deep sea between Aran and the mainland. Well, it would take over an hour to go from the mainland to this rock where the seaweed is growing. Between the walking and the boat trip, it was maybe three quarters of an hour.

We have this strapweed growing near us, but it's not very good. It grows broad, and out in the open sea it is slender, heavier, with more sap in it. The people of this area have no strapweed at all. They used to buy it from other people, from people who lived close to the sea, closer than we do and they own the strapweed. We have no strapweed but we had black weed on our own land. It comes with the land but we had no strapweed because there was none in the place where we have the black weed. There is only mud, that is, you know, mire. It's something soft. There are rocks there and perhaps this mud is about twenty feet deep. You would drown there, it's that soft.

When the water leaves it with an ebbtide, all of this mud is dry perhaps for a mile. It is so soft that even a seagull can barely walk on it. One doesn't get this mud or mire where the strapweed grows. It is washed by the strength of the sea. People often get stuck and they break their legs or hands by accident.

10 Old Shoe as Mock Man-of-War (Song)
Seán Ó Conghaile, Cnoc na hAille,
Indreabhán, Connemara

You were telling a story, do you know, about a man whose foot got caught in a fissure. There was a story like that around here about ninety or a hundred years ago. Do you see, it was before the bridges were built into the Connemara islands, into Leitir Mealláin, Leitir Móir and Béal an Daingin bridge. The people had no other way, but to walk out across the rocky foreshore and that was very dangerous especially when there was a spring tide. The tide would go out very quickly, you understand, but it would also come in very quickly. There wasn't any bridge until about the year 1890 when Balfour came. He was the leader, the Taoiseach, the Prime Minister of England at the time. That was the time when a lot of work was done here, you know. The bridges were built in Connemara.

There was a man from Cois Fharraige by the name of Mánus Mór (Big Mánus) going back one day, back to a place called Tráchta which is near Leitir Móir, between Leitir Móir and Tír an Fhia, or into the islands. He was going across the foreshore, walking, and it was ebb tide and the tide had gone out . But his foot went down between two stones as far as his boot and he was not able to pull it out. He was stuck.

He was afraid that he would be kept there until the tide would come in, so that he would be drowned, you know. What he did was to unlace his boot; he then pulled his foot out of it and he left the boot behind him in the rocky shore. But after a while, the tide going in and out, softened the boot and it came up and floated along. There was a man around then who composed a poem and here is some of it.

One shoe and one sock that went from Mánus
on Carraig na dTráchta and wasn't that an inconvenience.
Send news to Mac Maolra in Aran
to put it in the paper throughout the seven kingdoms.

The king's sloop is watching her since Wednesday morning
until they met with one another at the beach of Inis Oírr.
It wasn't the combat of the hag that they fought with one another
from the rising of the sun until it did set.

Powder was being scattered as if a snowstorm were blowing,
bullets were bursting and flying with the wind,
Here's what Captain Potter said to the vessel that was pursuing her
[the boot],
'Let her go or else she will kill the [whole] world.'

And there was much more in the song [but I only know]
another verse I think.

You neighbours of Garmna, you friends and you patrons,
you might do me a favour yet,
Search the stepping stones when the tide goes out,
and God knows you might find the boot.

I got that from people who are now dead. They are dead
for a long time, but I learned that much. Mánus Mór an
Chéidigh was the name of the man who lost the boot, but
they say that it was his father or his grandfather that composed the poem. But I am not sure.

11 Slippery Strapweed Mound Causes Drowning
Pádraig Ó Loideáin, Maol Rua, Maoinis, Carna

The man that drowned was from Roisín na Mainíoch; the incident occurred when he was in a boat, and I believe there was a mound of seaweed in her – a mound of strapweed. Val was his name, I'd say, yes. He went to move the boat from one place to another in order to take more seaweed and he happened to stand up on the top of the strapweed mound. He had a punt-pole and was shoving the boat over to this particular place, in order to take up the weed. The strapweed slipped out from under his feet and he went overboard and he didn't come ashore until he was found drowned. I think that he couldn't swim. If he had been able he was not far from the shore, you understand, that he couldn't have reached the land. It must have been that he couldn't swim.

Well, this same man was enlisted in the army in Galway, in Renmore Barracks, and his father went down and bought him out of the army. Perhaps it would be a small amount that would buy him at that time, you understand, but he bought him free and I believe he brought him home to work, is why he brought him home. I think he wasn't a fortnight at home when he was drowned. That's all I know about that now.

Question: He mightn't have been used to that kind of work, maybe?

Answer: Everyone around here had experience with that kind of work, but it was with hatred for that work that he left and enlisted. As I will tell you, ever since they were able to go out as children working with seaweed and everything else, they were doing it. They had no shoes or stockings either.

12 Drowning due to Excessive Load
Pádraig Ó Máille, Cor na Rón Láir, Cois Fharraige

Question: Did you ever hear of people drowning while gathering seaweed with a currach?

Answer: I did, but I was not born or in this world when it happened to two brothers in the village, may God have mercy on them now. They were cutting seaweed in that manner. Micil Ó Coisteala and Tomás Ó Coisteala were their names. And there are people belonging to them still living in this place. The two of them were coming back in a currach with a big load of seaweed cut. The place they were cutting the seaweed was a place they call 'Carraig an Rúin', in the next village. And they wanted to bring the seaweed near to the land in the village where they lived. There was a roundabout way by the sea to transport the load, but had they turned into the village where they cut the seaweed, they would have been saved. They were anxious to take the short cut to bring the seaweed to the village in which they lived. On their way back, the sea rose high and the day got kind of rough, and they then were ... they may have been a quarter of a mile from the land, from the shore.

They were keeping as close to the land as they could because they were overloaded and they were equally afraid that they might strike a rock and they wanted to stay reasonably deep for fear of hitting any rock. And the currach began to take in water, and what they did was to start throwing the seaweed overboard. They knew well that they had taken too much of it. The sea burst in on them, filling into the currach, and the currach sunk under their feet, and the two brothers were drowned. Neither of them could swim, but if they had been able they would have been able to make for the shore.

There were two others emptying a currach.

What they did was go on a rock cutting it [i.e. the seaweed]. They did not have the seaweed gaff, they did not have the big gaff [that they have] now for cutting the seaweed, but small oat sickles or knives. And they used to fill the seaweed from the rock straight into the currach. When it would begin to flow they would keep the currach afloat until they themselves would get into it. And then they put too much seaweed into the currach. And they did not have the big sickle with them that day — they used to bring out the big sickle when the day was fine and there would be no strand at all, do you know. There might be a weak spring tide. There might be no seaweed strand at all but they would be able to cut a currach full of seaweed and they would have a twelve-foot handle on the gaff that time, do you know. They used to be cutting down under them with the long handle that was on the gaff. But on that day did not have the gaff with them.

There were two others at the landing place and they emptying another currach of seaweed and when they saw the danger that the others were in, a little way back the way. They saw the currach sinking on them.

But they saw them from them, being drowned and he just tipped the currach in which he had the seaweed at the landing place and threw the seaweed out of it at once. He rowed back his currach to where they were being drowned. He came directly on top of them. He tried to catch a hold of one of them with one hand. His head came near him and he tried to grab it with one hand but it sank again on him. He failed to save either of them even though he came to them as fast as he could. He failed to save either of them after that, so that they were drowned, may God have mercy on them.

But do you know, they were buried at sea that time. But they say that a person like that rises, God help us, twice or three times and when he rose one particular time his head came so close to the man in the boat that he tried to grab his hair with his hand but he lost him after that. He failed to catch him.

13 *Climín* Drags Man off Pier
Peadar Ó Ceannabháin, Cill Chiaráin

It happened here about two years ago but the young man was not on the *climín*. But he got ... they brought this *climín* ashore. It was made, so to speak, ... in a place called Cuan Chamuis. And these two young men brought the *climín* ashore. Well I don't have their names now, I am not sure of their names.

But one of them went to fasten the boat and he sent the other man up on the pier. And there was a very strong current flowing up the bay. While the first man was fastening the boat, the other man went up on the pier and tied the rope to his leg — that was a foolish thing he did — trying to gain more support, so as to bring the *climín* in. And he wasn't strong enough to bring the *climín* in because the current was [too strong] — it had too much of a grip on it. It pulled him off the pier and he was drowned.

And when the other man came back, he saw that the *climín* was gone and there was no sign of the other young man. And he went to the neighbours, in a great hurry to find him and the *clímín* was found, stuck in a rock and this man's body in the bottom of the stony seabed. And it was he who was acting as anchor for the *clímín* when he was found drowned. That happened about three years ago in Snámh Bó.

14 The Sham Seaweed Raft Drowns Man
Áine Ní Choisdealbha (Aged 12), National School, Ros a' Mhíl

There was a man long ago and he was going fishing on this day. He got the boat ready. He wasn't long out when he saw an outline. He headed out towards it and when he was almost beside it, it appeared to him to be a raft of seaweed. The sort of thing a *clímín* is, is some sticks out from the end of the boat, with ropes up out of it. They used to fill seaweed onto the sticks and the ropes used to retain it. There used to be more than one boat-load on it then. They used to tie a big rope back at the end of the boat and pull it after them. But at any rate when he had to, he jumped in onto it and it took the man to the bottom of the sea. This man arises every seventh year and people see him. A man that took the great leap upon himself rises every seventh year.

15 Seaweed Raft, Crosspole, Inlet and Threshold
Peadar Ó Ceannabháin, Carna

Before there were any boats, it is said that that is how they travelled, so to speak, when they went gathering this seaweed, making the seaweed rafts. And a man would go up on the raft, when it would float, and he had a *croisín*, up to 18 feet in length. A *croisín*, that is a round piece of wood, about three inches in diameter and 18 feet in length. And ash wood is supposed to be the best for a *croisín*. And they used to stick the *croisín* in the raft, with a man on top, until they brought it ashore.

They even do it in Oranmore, Co. Galway, because there are beaches, and when the day is fine and the currents are favourable, they can bring them ashore with the *croisín*. Beside Oranmore in Galway, over beyond Galway, that is still done. The sea at Oranmore is very still, there's hardly any rough water, it's very far inland.

But the man who pushes the seaweed raft is in danger and indeed always has been. If he dropped the *croisín* ... and usually there was a fair bit of weight on him, trying to push the raft ... and went out after the *croisín* ... but if he held onto the *croisín*, if he couldn't swim, it would keep him afloat, until he could catch the raft again. Because, usually there was a man on the land, keeping an eye on him. But I don't remember seeing that being done, but I heard the old people saying, that that's the way it was in the olden days.

And even if there's a place, let's say, where there is an inlet with a threshold ... a threshold is the same as, sort of ... a place with a *crompán* inside and is deep. And the place ... the way out of it, outside it, is shallow, and we call that a *tairseach*. And [we also say] *tairseach an dorais* .... a narrow place, and that is the threshold. And often, perhaps, that the boat could not ... that she would not swim in, and that a man would have to go on the raft, and to shove out the raft from the threshold, until he would fasten it to the post of the boat, in order to pull it out.

16 Making and Transport of Seaweed Raft and its Breaking up by Storm
Peadar Ó Ceannabháin, Bantrach Ard, Cill Chiaráin

When we begin to cut this seaweed, the knotted wrack, we lay out our ropes to make the seaweed raft. When we have the ropes laid out and the seaweed cut, we gather the seaweed with our forks and we put it into the ropes. We don't make use of a sickle, but have a certain kind of knife, a seaweed knife. It is about ... it's not as big as a butcher's knife ... it's about nine inches altogether and ... there is a certain kind of whetstone, they call it a *cloch speile* (scythe-stone) which sharpens the knife. And the knife has to be sharpened very often, because you are cutting this seaweed off the rock and if the edge of the knife touches the rock, it loses its sharpness. They also use a sickle but it's not as good as the knife.

When that is cut, when the seaweed is cut, we put it into the ropes. And then, when we have it put on top of each other, or let's say, when we have all the seaweed gathered together and the raft is ready, we tighten the ropes around it. The rope is like a net on the raft. When that is done, the tide is coming in on us then, and we must prepare the raft with two ropes, with a mooring stone on each end of the rope, anchored on the stony shore, so that if a storm or a sea-swell should come, that the raft would not be swept away.

But it happens when the storm increases and when the tide goes out, and since the raft is made on a rough shore, with a sea-swell, it tears the lower part of the raft, hitting with the swell of the sea and the seaweed is swept away. It drifts away with the wind. The seaweed drifts with the current and scatters back and forth and it might come ashore on another rocky shore, ten or twenty miles away from where it was cut. In particular, this usually only happens in winter. When the weather is fine, we will try to bring these seaweed rafts ashore at the pier, as soon as the tide is suitable to pull the raft, because the raft must be pulled with the current. It is with a motorboat that these rafts are pulled. There is great weight in the raft, even from three tons to five tons. And it happens that, if there is a large group gathering seaweed, let's say four or five men, that the master of the boat pulls the other raft — that the other men have gathered — after his own, so that there are perhaps ten tons being pulled after the boat.

And we have to pull that, maybe about two miles and often three and a half miles of sea, and that takes us two and a half hours with the current, to come to where we are bringing these rafts. And it also happens when we are travelling to the pier, that a gale comes, and due to the swell and pull of the sea, that we lose some of the seaweed, tying it on the raft, except that we make an effort to [use] more ropes when we are pulling it, do you understand, to anchor the boat and pull the rafts, and we try to put other ropes around it, to retain it until we bring it to the pier. And that also often happens in winter.

And then, when it is brought to the pier, it is put in on a tractor and brought to the weighing bridge, until it is put into the factory, where it is put into a kiln. It is dried and made into meal. The meal is put in bags and the amount of meal in these bags is weighed, with about a half ton weight. And it is stored until the cargo boat from Scotland comes, until there are up to five hundred tons of this seaweed to be shipped to Scotland or to Holland or to wherever there is a market for it.

Question: (Regarding the mooring stone)
Answer: The mooring stone weighs about half a hundred weight ...

17 The Reason for the Name 'Na Foiriúin Bháite'
Peadar Ó Ceannabháin, Cill Chiaráin

There was another place called 'Na Foiriúin' — two submerged rocks. A very high tide would submerge them. It was a place people used to go long ago to pluck *creathnach*, or as some people call it — *duileasc. Creathnach* grew in abundance on Dubhleac and on Carraig na Meacan.

When the tide was out, the women went in to pluck this *creathnach*, or the *duileasc*. They were brought in there by boat and the men put them ashore, on the rocks. They went perhaps into Galway Bay. The sea got very rough.

Then when they came back, the sea was rough around these rocks and they were unable to go ashore, as there were shallow breakers around them. It was not possible to rescue these women as the boat could not go up as far as them. It is a shallow, wild place, which was very dangerous when the sea was rough.

When the tide rose, the rocks were submerged and the women were left on the rocks. They were looking at these from outside the island, being drowned. And that is the reason they have been called *Foiriúin Bháite* ever since.

18 Origin of the Name 'Caladh na gClimíní' (Landing-place of the Seaweed-rafts)
Val Ó Donnchadha, Bantrach Ard, Cill Chiaráin

The place you are in now, this house in Gort na gCapall, there is a landing-place back opposite this house, which they call the Landing-place of the Seaweed-Rafts. And it got this name because there is an island outside of it which we call Oileán an Chabhrnáin. There is an odd little bit of grass growing on the summit of the island, but has never been submerged by the sea as long as I can remember.

Our forebears who preceded us used to make seaweed-rafts. They used to cut seaweed ... Then they had two ropes, or a couple of tying strings and they would spread it out on the crossroad and then they would fill it with armfuls of seaweed and when they finished the raft, they tightened it.

And usually, often, a man was would stand in the centre of it. The way to the shore was not long, and he would place was given its name and it is called that ever since. shove it out with his long cross pole till he came ashore in the 'Landing-place of the Seaweed-Rafts'. That is how the landing place was given its name and it is called that ever since.

19 Creathnach-picking Girls on Rocky Islet Drowned by Tide
Máirtín Ó Domhnaill, Baile Thiar, Inis Oírr

I heard my mother say one time, relating a story about two girls from Baile an Luach in Co. Clare. They went down one morning under the big cliffs gathering *creathnach* and they did not return when it was time to do so and their father and mother and the rest of the family became worried. So they went to fetch them, but they found no trace of them.

And what happened was that they went out onto a rocky islet picking *creathnach*. The tide was coming in and they did not know it. The tide was turning and as they were eager picking the *creathnach*, they forgot about it, and the channel between them and the land inside, it filled up with water on them.

They were unable to come in then and had they gone into the water and tried to make it in initially, they would probably have saved their lives. But they thought all the time that help would come. In the end they were afraid. What happened in the end was that the two were drowned.

When they went searching for them, finding no trace of them anywhere, they realised that it was drowned they were. I think they were found drowned afterwards, days afterwards. The corpses were thrown up in on the shore.

And that's how it happened to them.

You would often see, back on the shore, if you were there, you would see a small piece as big as this kitchen and the room, a great, dry islet. And there would be water around it and you would have to go out in the water, up to your knees maybe, to get up on it. And the place was dry. They often cut seaweed, wrackweed, on top of the like and they call that a *creachoileán*.

Addendum to No 19

Then Donnán, son of Líath, a pupil of Senán's and two little boys who were reading along with him, went to cut seaweed for Senán on the shore (of a rock in the sea). (Donnán returned to Inis Cathaigh and) the sea carries off his boat from him, and he had no boat for the boys, and there as no other boat in the island to succour the boys. So the boys were drowned on the rock. Then on the morrow their bodies were borne (on the tide) till they lay on the strand of the island. Then came their parents and stood on the strand, and asked that their children should be given to them alive. Said Senán to Donnán: 'Tell the boys to arise and converse with me.' Said Donnán to the boys: 'Ye are permitted to arise and converse with your parents, for so saith Senán to you.' They straightway arose at Senán's orders, and said to their parents: 'Ill have ye done unto us, bringing us out of the land which we had reached.' 'Why', saith their mother to them, 'would ye rather stay in that land than come back to us?' 'Oh mother,' say they, 'though the power of the whole world should be given to us, and its delightfulness and joyance, we should deem it the same as if we were in a prison, compared with being in the life and the land which we reached. Delay us not; for it is time for us to go back to the land out of which we have come; and for our sakes God will cause that ye will not suffer sorrow after us.' Then their parents give them their consent, and they went along with Senán to his convent, and the Sacrifice was given to them, and they go to heaven; and their bodies are buried before the convent in which Senán abode. And those are the first dead folk that were buried in Inis Cathaigh. ('Life of Senán', Whitley Stokes, *Lives of the Saints from the Book of Lismore*, Oxford, 1890, p. 217)

20 Taboo of Retrieving Corpse from Sea Observed
Labhrás Ó Conghaile, Baile an Fhorma, Inis Oírr

A Joyce woman who lived back in Inis Meáin, herself along with two other neighbours, went down [to the shore] at Ceann an Bhrobh. There was a way down by the cliff. But there was a level flag below at the foot of the cliff and a lot of *creathnach* used to grow there. They went down and cut the *creathnach*. It was a low ebb tide. The tide had gone out from the cliff.

And as that was so, she stayed on. She told the other two to go home, I believe. But the other two neighbours left her while she remained. When she thought of coming up, something happened to her head — a faintness — and she fell. She did not regain consciousness until the tide was upon her and she drowned. Well, she didn't sink at all. She floated on top of the sea. The clothes were keeping her up. She didn't sink at all. She stayed on the top of the sea. She was met by a currach, but they didn't pick her up.

After a day or two or on the same afternoon — I am not sure which — a man from the island, Inis Oírr, was going out to Ceann na Faochan and he found her beside Ceann na Faochan, on the west side, just lying there nicely without any injuries, lying in on the flag. He brought her up. Her family came over, and there were people belonging to her as well, friends and relations from Inis Oírr also. Her name was Bríd Seoigheach. That's all there is to it.

Question: ... (As to why she was not picked up).

Answer: I don't know. I don't know. They were afraid or something. I don't know why. But I heard a Connemara man saying, whose name I didn't know either ...

Question: But what did you hear?

Answer: But I heard, if you'd believe it, that the same thing had happened to themselves and that they were not picked up by anyone ... that the same thing happened to themselves.

Question: And they alive or ...?

Answer: No, but drowned. They weren't able to save themselves.

Question: What do they say or believe?

Answer: It is said that it isn't lucky to rescue a person from the sea or to save a corpse from the sea. There is no merit in that. There is great merit to be got from saving someone — to bring him in safe, alive or dead.

21 Pregnant Girl to be Drowned on *Creathnach* Rock
Val Ó Donnchadha, Bantrach Ard
Cill Chiaráin

Women, who went to pick *creathnach* from the other side of the bay, on a rock out there which is called Dubh Leac. There were two brothers in the boat and they were going to cut *coirleach* with a cross-pole. They brought these women with them to pick the *creathnach*. Well, one morning at daybreak, they put the women ashore on the rock, and I do not know if it was Dubh Leac or not. But whatever rock it was, it used to submerge with the tide.

There was a young woman in the boat that day and one of the men, of the (two) brothers, had brought trouble on her and he wanted to get rid of her. And when he came back to fetch the women, he would not collect them, and his brother said to this woman: 'Oh woman,' he says,

'I will hide you in the space under the foredeck. You can put your head under the floor board and I might be able to save you.'

And so she did. And he (the brother) did not pick up the other women. He thought this (particular) one was among them. And when they came ashore on the other side of the bay (Cuan Chill Charáin), he only had the woman he had wished to drown and he did not have the other women at all.

'And I am alive,' says she, 'I had better [go away]. Long life to you!' says she to the brother, 'but I am alive in spite of you.'

And they returned [to the rock] and having done so the other women had drowned and their baskets floated away on top of the water.

— Chapter Two —

Adventures and Wonder Stories

22 **Diving to the Sea-bed to Release the Grapnel**
Val Ó Donnchadha, Bantrach Ard,
Cill Chiaráin

They used to pick it at Carraig Iolra. There was a crowd from Coill Sáile out and the man had a large hooker boat. Well, there were maybe seven or eight or however many women, men and children. The man had a large hooker boat and a small rowing boat tied to it, being pulled behind, in and out. Anyhow, when they had the *creathnach* gathered, they anchored the hooker boat out there in the deep ... down, the grapnel, to let down that anchor.

They were foolish, they were thinking that the place wasn't too strong, but what it was was a shallow rocky sea-bed covered with seaweed and it (the anchor) lodged where it couldn't be released. But they didn't know that, and they kept on gathering the *creathnach*. Well, about the middle of the day, the tide was out, about midday. They were gathering there ... *creathnach* ... until the tide was halfway in, and they were gathering up then, making for the boat, for to head for home. They had to put it in bags and to carry it on their backs to the small boat. For there is a harbour at Carraig Iolra which we call Caladh Charraig Iolra and it is a very still place, and let's say about twenty paces to the north of that, there is a place we call Leac Dhearg — Maidhm Leac Dhearg, it is rough and wild, and the sheltered side is there — it is very still.

But at any rate, they all went into the small boat and they loaded the *creathnach* on board the boat ... the big hooker boat. When they went to pull up the anchor, it was stuck.

'Ah,' said the man, he said, 'I will have to cut the rope.' But there was a young lad from Coill Sáile there, the poor man went to America and I think he died, the Lord have mercy on him. Micheál Dundas was his name, Michael Dundas.

'Ah, don't cut the rope,' says he, 'I'll release the anchor.'

'Ah,' says this man, 'you are out of your mind.'

'Not at all,' says he.

He sprung out over the breast hook and down he went. He wasn't long down when they heard the noise of the anchor being released from the stony sea-bed. He released the anchor from the stony sea-bed and he himself came to the surface and into the hooker.... But for that, he had lost the anchor. The young lad saved it. He was from Dúiche Sheoigheach, and his mother and father also. He wasn't very accustomed to the sea.

23 Marcas Lifted Six Hundredweight of Kelp
Val Ó Donnchadha, Bantrach Ard
Cill Chiaráin

Maybe it's up to a hundred years now. It's not a hundred years, but it's well over four score since that man ... oh I am not able to say ... there is nothing else to say about him, but that he was a good man, that he was very strong: Marcas Ó Ceannabháin from Aill na Brún.

Well, kelp was being weighed in Cill Chiaráin, at one time, and there was a man from across the bay, from Doirín Glas the man was. He was a big strong man and he took a strong kelp piece, weighed on the weighing scales, five hundredweight. He put it in on the scales.

'That's one thing, now,' says he, 'that I have done that no other man in the community will do, save I.'

But the man who was in charge of the kelp, Pat Dick we used to call him, he enquired for the man. He asked for him and he came. And 'By dad, Marcas,' says he, 'the people are humiliated,' says he, 'if you are not any good of a man.' 'What do you mean?' says my father. He told him.

'Ara,' says he, 'that's nothing.'

He lifted the scales three more links. And Marcas Ó Ceannabháin got hold of a stone of kelp and he told him to put another stone on top of it and that was six hundredweight and he had no bother letting it down onto the scales.

'Now,' says he, 'is there any man in the community,' says he, 'who will do that?' And there wasn't, save himself. That's all there is about that now.

24 **Conroy Woman Shifts Stranded Boat, Carries Five Hundred and Fifty Pounds' Weight of Kelp**
Mícheál Mac an Iomaire, An Cuillín, Cill Chiaráin

When they used to have the kelp burnt around here — during the kelp season long ago — their practice often was that a man who owned a big boat or a reasonably big boat, perhaps three or four people would bring their kelp to Caiseal or Cill Chiaráin or to Roundstone. Anyhow, this particular day, two men had to send some kelp of theirs to Caiseal and they went to speak to a man who had a big boat and he took their kelp off them and they made for Caiseal. There were five or six altogether in the boat. And there was a woman also, she was in the boat.

At any rate, they had a heavy cargo and the boat went aground on a rock with the darkness of the night. So each one of them had to go out under the boat to try and shift her off the rock and, by dad, it was failing them to remove her.

'To hell with you all,' said the woman, 'it can't be that we will be kept here until morning,' [says she], going out under the boat. When the woman went out, she put her shoulder to the boat and pushed it off the rock. It was a big job to get the boat off the rock as the tide was ebbing.

At any rate, they made their way to Caiseal with the kelp. They arrived early in the night but there was to be no kelp weighed until the following morning. The way kelp was that time, it used to be in big slabs. Perhaps there would be as much as 500 pounds in one piece of kelp. Maybe another piece would only be half a hundredweight or a hundredweight. At any rate, a particular big piece, had been put into the boat. I think three or four men had been loading it into the boat. And they said they wouldn't like to break it. One of the men that was in the boat asked, 'Do you think there is anybody in the boat' said he, 'who would carry this piece of kelp?'

There was a big strong man there, of the Burke family, and he said that he would try himself to carry it. He was only gone six steps with it from the boat when he said to the other men that he was not able for it and to support him. The two were asked if there was anyone able … 'Well,' said the woman, 'there is no one who can carry it, nor able to try, but I will try,' said she. She was one of the Conroys. And they hoisted it up on her back and she didn't rest and she didn't sigh until she left it on the kelp weighing scales. She brought it well over a good hundred yards. This portion of kelp was laid down on the scales and what it weighed were five hundred and fifty pounds. It was reckoned to have been the heaviest weight ever carried by a woman around here.

But what she was … she was a great woman in every way. She was better than any man. She was able to drink poteen wherever drink was to be had and she was able to drink black stout also. When every man was ready and the kelp was weighed and everyone paid, they went into the public house. There were six or seven men. Each one of them was getting a drink in his turn, and the woman herself was calling for a drink also. Soon the men were for the most part, they were not able to drink anymore and they were half drunk. The woman herself drank fifteen pints of porter. She carried some of the men on her back and threw them into the boat, and it was she who sailed it home.

[Discussion of the woman follows]
Ciarán Mac an Iomaire: Who was that woman?
Micheál Mac an Iomaire: She was a sister of Beartla Conroy.
Ciarán: Which of them was she?
Micheál: I can't say now.
Ciarán: I also heard talk about her, but I have forgotten it. Wonderful, wonderful, she was really good.
Micheál: You could say indeed that this woman was strong.

Ciarán: I heard my own father say that he himself carried five hundredweight of kelp.

Micheál: He did, his father carried that, five hundred. Wasn't it Hazel who was dealing with the kelp at that time?

Ciarán: It was.

Micheál: Do you think he was a Scot?

Ciarán: I know he was a Scot.

Micheál: She was able to work the crosspole. She could ride a horse and everything. She was one day going to an island. The horse was able to walk all right, but on her way out, as she was eyeing the cattle there, the tide had come in, she made the horse swim out and what the devil did the horse do, but — whether it was the spray went into its eyes — anyhow, the horse made for the sea. And only for two men who were on the beach in a currach, the devil a sight of her would be seen ever again.

25 Dog Takes Seaweed News Home
Willy Ó Conghaile, Baile Thiar, Inis Oírr

Long ago, at the time of the kelp-making, up to maybe thirty years ago, there was a man in the village above called John an Muimhneach (John the Munsterman). This day he went out to the shore to see if he could find any seaweed.

He went out the road — it was in May — and when he was near the shore, he saw a large amount of seaweed down on the dry shore.

And when he saw it, he went down and gathered it together, and he did not know then how to get the news home.

Anyhow, up and down, he thought of a plan. He took his handkerchief out of his pocket and he put two or three wisps of seaweed into it and he tied it well and tight around the dog's neck. He gave the dog a few good slaps to make him afraid, and he let him go and by dad, he headed for home, in the Béal an Chalaidh road.

That was all right. The dog was making his way and he met two or three people on the road and the dog jumped the wall from them and he came out on the road again when he found them gone. The dog was very clever.

As he was going in by Leac Cránail, he saw another man coming out the road, and so he went into Máirtín Folan's crag. He was coming in the road till he reached Bóthar an Chlaí Mhóir, and he did not meet anyone along that stretch till he got in home. When he lay down on the floor, the woman saw the handkerchief around his neck and she did not know why it might be there. She removed the handkerchief from the dog, and the dog did not move. She saw the fresh seaweed in the handkerchief and she knew where her husband went. She knew that he had gone to the shore to look for seaweed, for some kelp.

She quickly called two of the lads, Peadar and Pádraig. That was all right, they came.

'Do you see,' says she, 'what's round the dog's neck? There's a chance that he himself has a good lot of seaweed at Béal an Chalaidh.' And they got the baskets ready and the sheepskin and they brought a few baskets with them. That was all right, while he was out there, all the time, sitting by the shore, he was thinking, but nobody was coming to him.

After two or three hours they came and they had a few baskets with them and they brought out tea and loaves of homemade bread with them also. They worked up the seaweed and brought a good amount of it up above the highwater mark, to keep it from the tide. The seaweed comes in all the time with the tide. With the flood tide the seaweed comes to every shore. The ebbtide brings the seaweed out, but even if it does, the flood tide brings it in again. Especially with a north wind a lot of seaweed comes on the south side.

And by dad, they brought it up and they got great drying for the seaweed. And when that amount was up and the tide in, they had the other heap up above the highwater mark and they were bringing that up to the spreading ground everywhere, the seaweed for the kelp. By dad, when they had that much brought up, they had tea again the second time and they finished all the tea they had. The following day there was again a heavy layer of seaweed on the same shore, but there were [also] more people there the following day.

On the south side, a lot of weed comes in because the mayweed is to be got out on the south shore. They put up about a ton of kelp in the two days. That was about seven pounds, and it was difficult to earn seven pounds at that time. And they got the drying with it and the north wind. And that's the end of the story.

26 Calemelassity: a New Word for *Coirleach* (strapweed)
Val Ó Donnchadha, Bantrach Ard, Cill Chiaráin

A stranger came here, a good few years ago. The old people, who are now on the way of truth, God be good to them, were alive at that time. I was only a young lad, like my brother Michael. He was a very witty boy. I did not have any English nor did he either, unless we had the odd word.

Anyhow, there was a man over in Aill na Brún, a relation of our own, and Michael used to make up things always for him, foolish things, and he used to believe him, quite often, the two of us.

The man from over there (Aill na Brón) was a smith. He was a first cousin of my mother, Pádraic Ó Ceannabháin. But Michael said to him: 'There was a stranger back at our place, Pat,' he said.

'Well, was there, dear?' he said.

'There was,' he said.

'Who was he?'

'Oh, I have no idea,' says he, 'some big buck from England,' he says. 'He and Val were discussing with one another, talking about seaweed and asking what was the English for *feamainn dubh* and for *feamainn bhuí* and everything. 'At last,' he said, 'he asked Val what we call *coirleach* in English.'

'Val was thinking to himself,' he says, 'and he didn't know from the devil what he would say, because he did not have the English,' says he, 'nor the grammar,' says he. 'Then he thought of a good plan.'

'Well, Sir,' he said, 'the English name we have for *coirleach*, we call it calamelassity, *coirleach* growing on the rocky shore.'

'He said that now, Michael, did he?' says Paitín.

'He did,' says my brother.

'Oh well,' he said, 'may he be seven times worse in a year's time a year from tonight.' 'Isn't it he has no shame,' says he, 'the thief of a beggar, speaking English to an Englishman.'

[It is Michael who invented the word *calamelassity* — it is a combination of two English words: **calam**-ity and nec-**essity**.]

27 'Upon My Soul, We Would Eat the Neap Tide Itself'
Pádraic Mac Donnchadha, Ros a' Mhíl

He [this man] used to be coming out to the mountainous bogland with his cattle and usually he brought some dulse [edible seaweed] along for them [some friends]. Anyway, he came out on this day. The people of Connemara used to put out their cattle on the hill for grazing, up the mountainous bogland. Indeed they still do.

Anyway, this particular man used to come to a special farm and left some cattle for grazing there every winter.

He used to bring dulse for the house every time he came there.

He came there on this particular day, but he had no dulse [with him].

'You have no dulse at all today,' said the head ... the man of the house.

'Ah, there is no spring tide now,' says he, 'there is only,' says he, 'a neap tide.'

'Upon my soul, we would eat the neap tide itself,' says he. He thought that was also dulse.

28 Astray in Fog
Seosamh Ó Flatharta, Baile an Chaisleáin, Inis Oírr

Three people from here who went out fishing long ago, I suppose, it must be about sixty years ago. I don't remember it, but that I heard it from Joyce. And they were out with longlines in spring. And at that time there was not much bread or flour to make bread which they could take with them in the currach, nor did they use much tea, I believe, at that time, as it was not very plentiful.

When they went out in the morning, they took with them in the currach, it is likely, a piece of boxty cake. They were out to the south of the island, maybe the tower eastward from the lighthouse, or some place like that.

They cast the longlines and they pulled them in again. When they had the lines almost in, a fog closed in on them. When that happened, they did not know where they were then. Well, I suppose they thought they were heading towards home. The three were rowing away. The day was fine and calm, sure enough, for there is never a foggy day that is not calm. There was not a puff of wind.

They were rowing away thinking that it was for home that they were making. After a few hours there was no sign of home, there was no sign of the island. And whatever little bread they had, they had eaten it. The man rowing at the back of the currach, he said: 'Well now, we are getting hungry, and I am worn out. I am almost knocked out with the hunger and I am not able to do any more. And since I am not, it is a great pity that the three of us should die,' he said. 'Since I am so bad that I will not do any good, you had better draw my blood and drink it. It will bring the two of you home,' he said, 'and so only one of us will be lost. If you do not do that we will all perish. The three of us will be lost, the three of us will die with the hunger. And,' he said, 'There is no better plan in the world but that.'

'Here, take the knife and draw my blood,' he said to the man who was in the middle of the boat. This is the man at the back, you see, who was in a bad state. And as luck would have it, did it not clear a little, the fog lifted a little. And when it did, they found themselves just at the point of Ceann an Bhrobh in Inis Meáin.

They turned in then towards to the land as best they could. The man at the back, the poor man, was not able to do anything, as he was half-dead with the hunger. But the other man did not do as he said to him, he did not draw his blood. As luck would have it, outside the Cromail in Inis Meáin, there is a fine smooth rock, which is called the Rock of the Moss. And what was growing there on the rock, or around it somewhere, but a fine patch of *creathnach*.

'Well now,' said the man at the back, 'all we have to do is reverse in,' said he, 'to reverse the currach in and go ashore and we will eat our fill of the *creathnach* and that will be sufficient to bring us home.'

They reversed the currach in onto the rock and they pulled up the currach a little bit from the tide and the three of them went plucking and eating the *creathnach*. They ate their fill of it, and when they had eaten enough they were full up, as there is food in the *creathnach*, do you know, it is strong and it is food at the same time. It is called seashore food. When they had eaten enough of it, they launched the currach again and they got into it and they did not stop until they reached the beach here. But only for the fog lifted and they saw Inis Meáin, it is likely that the three of them would have been lost.

29 Porter and Songs instead of Burning Kelp
Peadar Seoighe, Baile an Fhorma, Inis Oírr

It was the custom long ago when kelp was to be burned, do you understand, you would have to bring out a drink for the men who would be with you, who would be helping you. Well, perhaps at the beginning there might be only one or two, do you understand, you wouldn't need any more.

Anyhow, there was poor Joe — of course Joe always liked a drop. He brought back what we used call a jar. That was like a big jug, made of clay, do you understand, it would hold five gallons. Of course, it was easy to buy it (the porter), eighteen pence a gallon. It was brought back to the house, put into a sack and they brought it out to the shore. The kiln was made and they were getting ready. There were four or five of them.

'Ah, here,' said Joe, 'give me the mug. We'll have a drop first.'

He handed round a mug to every man and they drank it and having done so, it seemed that they were all right.

'Ah,' said Joe, 'we'll have another one.' But they were like the little mouse long ago when it tasted the poteen, you see. It did not like the first drops but it put its tongue in it again, and it was somewhat better. But what did Joe do?

'We'll have another one,' said Joe.

Of course, you know yourself, three mugs and to drink them pretty quickly, when you are going to work, didn't it stir them up. And there was one old man yonder … There was no talk of lighting the kiln.

There was a certain old man there. 'Ah,' says he to Joe, 'you had better give us a tune. [Maybe] sing 'An Droighneán Donn' or another song.' So the songs started, the tunes started. When they did, there was no talk of [kelp]-burning. Another mug went round. But finally they were not able to light the kiln, or the seaweed.

'Ah,' says one man to another, 'we had better head for home, or if we light it, it will be ourselves who will be in it, instead of the seaweed, as it may seem,' he says.

So they decided to go home though the night was fine. But when they had come in the road a bit, weren't the women going out, you know, out with the supper, plenty of tea and bread. And when the women saw them;

'Ah, what's up or what sent you in?'

'Ah,' says the old man and he didn't let on anything. 'Didn't the wind change. The smoke was being blown towards the stacks of weed and you wouldn't have an eye in the morning .'

'Sure, if that's the case,' they said, 'hadn't we better turn back.'

'Oh, you had better turn back, you had better turn back,' says the old man, 'as there will be another night, please God. Pity him who would die on the bad day. Patience is good,' he said.

What kind of plan did the old man have, but that he would have another jar in a few day's time. And all you had to do was to keep drawing (porter) from the pub. That was the custom, and when you had burned the kelp, you would pay for it. But I don't know, I won't tell a lie, whether they brought out the second jar. But indeed I am sure, if they had five gallons the first night, that they were improving, so that they might have six gallons and if there was a third night, they would have ten gallons, I'd say.

30 Don't Mind the Flies — They are Some of Your Ancestors
Peadar Seoighe, Baile an Fhorma, Inis Oírr

This particular day, we were burning kelp, do you understand, out at the shore, and the poor old burner was there and another neighbour from the village, alongside him. His wife came with the dinner, and when she did, to give her her due, she laid it out.... We used to have a little corner for shelter. We'd sit there eating it (the dinner). Anyhow, the woman came with the tea. Indeed, you could say, that she had a basket. As for loaves, they were six inches high, some of them, maybe even a little more. Upon my soul, the crusts used to be burnt on some of them. But even though it was burnt itself, you'd eat it, if you were hungry.

Anyhow, she set it down there, a fine dish of fresh butter which she had just made. She had done the churning, the poor woman. When they do the churning at home, here, they put some salt in it. Ah, there's a fine taste on it, you know, and with this [...] and the smoke on you, like any man, you would crave a pint of porter, you understand.

She came down and laid the basin there, with the butter and bread and when she was cutting the bread, I was called out. As it happened, there was a man to spare; only two or three could go away from it at a time and two or three later. Anyhow, we got a small mug [of tea] and a few fine pieces of bread, and upon my soul, one could say that I was hungry and craved for it. She had a dock leaf to protect the butter from the sun, because in hot weather like that, it melts. When she took [the dock leaf] off the butter, she was working with the knife to butter the bread. She gave a piece to the old man and to the other man and then she gave me a piece.

And you know these cursed flies which are on the seaweed — whatever they find in it, they get the taste of the salt water or some other taste in it — anyhow, didn't a load of them land on the butter.

There was one of the old [men and he said], 'Bad luck to you,' says he, ' get out of that, get out of that.'

'Aren't I telling you,' says the other old man, 'don't mind them, the poor creatures.' 'Don't mind them,' says he, 'they are some of your own people.'

Oh sure you know, we all started laughing, pretending to believe it, when we thought of the poor flies. And we have it, ever since, do you understand, not to bother the flies. But indeed, I'm telling you, if we get our chance, we'll show the fly, if it comes around again, whatever about anything else.

31 The Fight of the Two Master Burners
Peadar Seoighe, Baile an Fhorma, Inis Oírr

We were this one day over at the shore. I myself was young and it was the fashion when you would go burning the kelp that time, like any other trade, you would need the burner. Anyway, the man whom I was with, he had got a burner. And there was another, about one hundred yards away from us, and he himself was also burning and he had another burner. They carried on working through the night, the creatures, but you know, in the morning, the following day, we went cleaning the kiln. The man that I was with, was going to start work before the other man, and what do you say, didn't the other old man come up. And you know that two burners are better than one. Oh, the pair were very sporting. And the bottle was there — when this burner came up he got a drop — and by my soul, the man for whom he was doing the burning had plenty of poteen, for he was selling it. We began working, as you would say, raking. But the two old men were more inclined to make fun. You'd think that the kiln wasn't causing them any worry due to the drop they had taken — the poor kiln man ... [was worried].

'Oh,' says he, 'look out for your work, I am afraid that I won't have anything from it, because it is very dry. Work it through.'

'Ara, what are you saying,' said one of the old men, 'are you going to tell me my business?'

'Ah, you clown, work it through!'

'Ara,' said he, 'if you don't leave me alone I will put this [raking bar] into your belly,' said he, 'it is red hot.'

The poor kiln man had to run because the [old] man was half-drunk, do you understand. He followed him with the red hot raking bar for fifty yards, and we had to go over to get a hold off him and bring him back. After that we calmed him down again. In spite of all that, however, we made grand kelp then. We made fine kelp of it and we settled a stone on it and everything was right. Then we sat down and we were talking. The bottle went around again — another couple of glasses, you know.

That was good. We went down then to the other man. There was a great welcome for us at that kiln and they themselves were almost finished. It had been burning for two nights. The burner that he had — except when he was with us — the poor man sat down and he was only sitting on the stone, and what do you say, with the drop he had taken, didn't his two eyes close with the sleep. Somebody suggested to leave him up in the seaweed for a little while. And you know the seaweed, we shook it up and we covered [him]. He had gone over there by himself, you know. We ourselves had told him to go there. And he stretched himself, even though he could hardly stretch, as the two eyes of the poor man were nearly closed, even before he went at all. But he stretched out (all the same). In a short time he began snoring for himself.

But he wasn't long there when the flies gathered, some in the ears, some in the nostrils, I'm telling you, whatever about his sleep, the fly didn't leave him long until he woke up. But we shook it [the seaweed] up again. Oh, indeed, you could say that the flies were cursed at, that day. But the poor man didn't have much of a chance. The kiln was due to be shaken up, you understand. We used to shake it up, always, when we were finishing, to shake it, or to rake it.

We started working and there was no word of sport then. We finished it then and we came home. Well, I myself came home. The owner of the kiln was calling us, but we didn't go there, because if we did go, we would have two more hours spent, eating a big pot of potatoes, you know, and fish and milk and talking with them, the creatures, the old men.

Well, the poor old man, the burner that Neidín had, he wasn't actually burning, maybe he was going back and forward to a lot of the neighbours, the creature, the poor man. Indeed he didn't get any sleep for a fortnight. You know the smoke, the heat, and the drink, there is nothing worse. You could be talking about doctors giving you drugs, this is the thing that would make you sleep, I'm telling you. You couldn't describe it, the effect on the head and on the stomach. The poor man was laid over in the seaweed. Oh, the devil, he didn't need any laying over, because it didn't matter where he was laid at that time. He was laid over in the seaweed, anyway, so that the poor man's two eyes and two ears would be away from the sea, anyway, so long as he wouldn't be smothered. I'm telling you that he was snoring. As Joe used to say long ago in the story: 'He was bringing the rafters down with every snore he was drawing.'

32 Selling Weed in Kinvara
Peadar Seoighe, Baile an Fhorma, Inis Oírr

There was another day here, indeed you have me killed talking about the same seaweed, and bad cess to it; it was what killed us, through everything. We were wet from when we'd rise until we'd go asleep.

There were two men here, a young man and an old man. They were in partnership, and as they were, the creatures were working away. When you would have a good boatload of seaweed saved, and when you would gather it in stacks, the old people used to say that that amount, if you burned it, would make perhaps a half ton of kelp for you.

Anyway, the turf boat came in this particular day. 'Well,' said an old man, 'if we are waiting for a month or a few months to burn it, a lot of it will be gone bad. But wouldn't it be the best thing for us to do, today,' said he, 'to go and load it, seeing that the boatman is willing to take it.'

'Come on then,' said the younger man.

They got the currach. Of course, they had help, I believe. They were not too long loading it, and they put all they had in it. Indeed they had a fine load of seaweed all right.

The day was fairly fine. The boat did not have much wind. But they were struggling on till they reached Black Head. When they were approaching Black Head, it was getting rather late in the evening. But the breeze improved then. They reached Kinvara, but it was very late. Ah, it was ten o'clock, I would say, or perhaps eleven. Most of the people of the village were asleep and they said that it was no good to go up through the village that night, that there was no chance that they would sell it.

'Oh,' said the Aran man, 'that will do.'

'Don't be afraid at all,' said the boatman, 'there will be plenty of people down here in the morning as soon as you will get up.'

But you know, perhaps, the Aran people are not used to being in these boats and they don't fall asleep as quickly as the boatman. The boatman need only stretch out and lay his head on the memory board and he is snoring.

But of course, alas, the boatman was worried, the poor man. He was up fairly early in the morning even though the place was safe, but that he wanted to see how the day was, and things, here and there. But he was not long up when there was a man coming down the quay wall.

'God bless,' he said to the boatman .

'God and Mary bless you,' said the boatman.

'You have a fine load of seaweed,' said the countryman.

'Well indeed yes, the best of seaweed. She never carried as much before,' said the boatman.

'Is there anyone with you.'

'There is no one with me,' said the boatman. 'It belongs to me.'

'How much do you want for it.'

'Well ....' So much.

'Oh, you are able to ask the price of your goods,' said the countryman.

'Upon my soul, if you were selling yourself, you probably would be able to ask your price,' said the boatman.

The two were arguing like that with one another. The old man from Aran, the poor man, was worn out from working the two days before that. Didn't he put his head up from the front hold. And you know, all the old men long ago, they were not as neat and tidy that time. They didn't shave themselves. He had a beard and was looking very dirty, the creature, and he was tired from loss of sleep.

'Ah,' said the countryman, when he saw him putting up his head, 'I think you have nothing to do with the seaweed, boatman,' says he. 'I think it belongs to the little razorbill from Aran.'

'Oh, bad luck to you,' says the Aran man, the razorbill from Aran.

Out came the old man, on the pier. Instead of selling the seaweed, what did he want but to fight. He was a good man to go selling. Upon my soul, it is difficult to sell anything when you go fighting. I'm telling you that farmer moved away fast. But it was not long after that again indeed until two or three others were down.

They sold the seaweed. Well I'm not sure now what they got, but they got a good price for it anyhow. The poor old man was satisfied. That's all there is about it.

33 Burning the Poor Widow's Kelp
Peadar Seoighe, Baile an Fhorma, Inis Oírr

This was the kelp season and all the people were preparing to burn the seaweed. It was to be bought in a fortnight or three weeks time. But the way it was, there were plenty of people on the shore and they were very close to each other and as they were, only one man could be burning every day. Because if there was a man on the wind side of you, all the smoke would be coming on top of you and your eyes wouldn't stand it. And the other man would have to ... he would have to stop. So the first man who was out would have the first chance.

Well, we were all at mass on Sunday and the weather was looking good. And as it was, we came home and there was a lot ... But the people of the islands don't really like to work on holidays. But this man went out and he lit a small fire. But he was doing nothing. He had occupancy of the place and no other man could go there. But' when late evening came, he called for help, he asked another man to come out. They lit up then [the kiln] at about ten or eleven o'clock. And they were burning away.

They hadn't it long lit, and the kiln was going, when the wind changed to the north east and it began to rain. And indeed I'm telling you that it was terrible. But they were barely able to keep it lit. But as the rain was heavy, it softened the seaweed and soaked it, and it wasn't burning too well. But at any rate they kept it going till morning, and the day cleared up and they threw the seaweed and they began to spread it out and they were doing very well throughout the day. But late in the evening on Monday, they had to clean the kiln. And they called for me. I went out to give them a hand. We got the kiln ready and we fixed it up well, and it was working well again. We brought it up and it was doing well.

But on Tuesday morning, we were well finished at about nine or ten o'clock. The man's wife came up to us on Tuesday morning and we were absolutely worn out, as we were up for two or three nights. She left down for us a large basket of bread, to do her justice, butter, mugs and everything. She saw a small heap of seaweed which was fairly well rotten, little cocks of laceweed and there was plenty of maggots in them, and she didn't like that much to go to waste. What did she do but go over and she caught one of them. And you know yourself, when the seaweed had been well burnt like a big turf fire and it nearly gone out. The kiln was well lit up, and there was this hole there and what does she do but throw this cock and the maggots and all that was there, down in this hole.

'Oh, bad luck to you,' said one of the men, 'after we killing ourselves, look at what she has done. She will quench it (the kiln) again.'

The man in my company drinking tea shouted, 'But what are you doing?' says he.

'Ara, what am I doing?' says she.

'Can't you see the amount that is going to waste here.'

'Oh, bad luck to you,' says he.

'Ah,' says he, 'after we being here, for three nights,' says he.

Well, if she quenched the kiln, you understand, with heaps such as these, the seaweed wouldn't burn properly. We would only have what we call dust or ash. It wouldn't melt properly or very well, you understand. She threw down the heap.

'You don't understand at all, how we have been. You are trying to destroy again what we have done,' says he. 'Don't you know,' says he, 'that nothing will burn that.' But that was nothing! Wasn't she going to pick up another heap. 'Oh here,' says he, 'go away. Get away from the kiln.' If we didn't have fun. The poor woman was trying maybe, to add a half hundredweight into it, you understand, you know, when she would have it all burnt. But anyway, didn't we bring her over again.

'Here,' he said to her, 'come over here, this is your job,' picking up a large loaf. Oh, she had a big knife! She started to cut the bread, but indeed she was a good generous woman, to tell the truth.

But when we had drank the tea, the day didn't do us any good. After that, it turned out that we couldn't burn everything. Didn't he say, 'Some other day will come when the sun will shine, and maybe you will spread [i.e. dry] that and you will burn it and that you would make small heaps,' says he, 'and it would be just as good,' said he.

But we had great fun. But we finished it anyway, and indeed we did a good job of it. But indeed, when we came home, you could say that we didn't need any bed, it didn't matter if it were sitting on a stool or in the corner of the fire place, smoky or not. We had our eyes closed going in the road, after three nights, you know, intense heat affecting the eyes, and the smoke was also bothering the eyes. But we went down and indeed even if we did, she brought us to the house again. If there wasn't poteen going around! We burnt what was there, about three or four tons. I'd say about three and half tons, anyhow, to four tons. She asked me how much I thought was in the kiln when we were finished.

'Well now,' says I, 'it is three feet wide, and it is an old kiln, says I, and its walls are nearly coming apart, it is three and a half feet wide. I would think,' says I, 'that you will have from three and a half ton to four tons.'

She herself was thinking — for she had great knowledge concerning stacks of seaweed — that there were three tons there, on the scales perhaps. But when I myself said four tons, didn't I receive two glasses, do you understand. The poor woman was so delighted. But that didn't please her, that wasn't enough for her. She had a big pot of potatoes down. Oh, by Jove indeed! She had a big salted fish up in the chimney, you know, dried eel. Oh, and the new potatoes, new potatoes at that time! Of course, the great taste was on their mouths. And indeed we started eating and if we didn't eat supper and a large piece of the dried eel. And milk! As for milk, it was there in every way. We had milk from the churn and she was after milking the cow, if you wanted a mug of it.

But I myself came home, and there is no lie there, maybe you won't believe it, I was dead out, tired. I went to bed at three o'clock on Tuesday afternoon and make what you like of it, I don't know if I opened them (i.e. my eyes). Maybe I did, but if I opened them, I didn't rise until it was eight o'clock on the following day. But I counted the hours, when my memory came to me ... seventeen hours exactly. It would do any man for a fortnight. But they used to say always, you understand ... my mother would nearly say about me ... often when I used to go to sleep, or if anyone came in to call on me, 'he is asleep and he is asleep for this long,' she says, 'And indeed, he would sleep in any manner, if his two eyes or his two ears were over sea level, or out of the water at all,' she said.

34 Yarn about the Seaweed-rafts in Kinvara
Val Ó Donnchadha, Bantrach Ard, Cill Chiaráin

There was an old man here, I was telling you before, Séamus Ó Ceannabháin. We used to be talking about seaweed rafts as you and I are doing now. He spent a good deal of his life over there, down in Munster, digging potatoes, it seems, when he was a young man. He was a very sporting and humorous person. He used to make up stories for us about things that never happened. He was telling us that he saw, over in Kinvara, people who were making seaweed rafts. When they had made them, they would let them go with the tide. And they would have a fire made in the middle of the seaweed raft and with one foot over the other, smoking their tobacco. It never happened but he was able to make them up — the funny ones.

— Chapter Three —

GAINS AND LOSSES

35 **Kelp Thrown Overboard**
Peadar Seoighe, Baile an Fhorma, Inis Oírr

The day turned bad, on this particular day, when we were going out with the kelp. Well, the wind went to the northwest and we had to tack. From Ceann Gainimh we had the first tack, we were brought to Trá an Tobair, nearly, that is, to the east of Ceann an Bhóthair. And turning west again, she was taking water and a lot of water. The poor boatman was tired working the bailer, bailing water.

'God help us,' said the man who was steering the boat. 'We will never keep her clear of water. Aran man, would you give him a hand for a little while?'

I caught hold of the bailer, I put it down and brought it up filled. And if you didn't take care of the handle of the bailer, you would break it on the side of the boat, when you put it on the side of the boat, you would break it. Ah, I did not understand it myself; but he asked me to be careful of the bailer.

'Ah well,' he says. She took another load of water. 'There is nothing else to be done,' he says, 'kelp will have to be thrown overboard.' When that was so, mine was out near the mast. I did not like to throw it overboard.

'Well, what I will do now', he says, 'is to throw overboard a half ton or fifteen hundredweight belonging to each one of you.'

The throwing out began. But indeed ... we were not able to put it out, but, of course, it was better to put it out and that we should save our lives. We put out about two tons and when he had done so, the boat was able to survive well. Of course, we had to tack westward again, almost in to Árainn Mhór and out again over Ceann Gólaim. The wind changed a little to the west and so it was a fair wind, and she was able to survive well. When I reached Cill Chiaráin I cursed kelp forever. We barely took the lower net-ropes with us (we barely got away).

36 Seaweed-laden *Púcán* Breaks in Two
Val Ó Donnchadha, Bantrach Ard, Cill Chiaráin

There is a place ... from my father, God rest his soul, I heard it. They were related to him, they lived back in Aird Mhóir, the Lawrence family, the Lawrences they used to call them. They were brothers. They had a fine *pucán* and were out one day, at a place near Carraig na Meacan, which they called Na Foiriúin. It is a very wild place, even in summer if there is any swell in the sea.

This particular day, they were out and they sailed the *púcán* in where no man had ever brought a boat, before or after them. They brought it in to the Foiriúin rock. That is what we call it. And they brought her in and they put props underneath her and they began to load her with tufted, red seaweed. But there was another man from Aird Mhóir, a neighbour of theirs. He himself was out also. He didn't go on the shallow. He didn't take the risk. His boat was loaded and he was waiting for them outside. And he said to them, 'Well,' says he, 'Lawrence, if you don't take out the seaweed you'll lose the boat. Maybe you'll lose your life.' 'I will not,' says he, 'nor devil a bit. I will not put out the seaweed,' says he. 'Well, you had better,' says he (the neighbour). But he didn't. They left the seaweed in the boat. Then a man by the name O'Flaherty came. He was originally from Leitir Mealláin, but married into Aird Mhór. We used to call him Máirtín Phaddy, God rest his soul. He was an able man.

'Well,' says he, 'seeing that you are not taking my advice....' He was lying at anchor a good distance from him, maybe twenty yards out on the deep. He had cast out the anchoring stone and what did he do but jump into the sea from his own boat and swim in towards the boat in Dug na bhFoiriún.

'Would you take my cable now?' says he. He put this heavy grapnel on his shoulders and swam out as far as the scope of this rope would let him. When the rope was used up, O'Flaherty let go. He dropped the grapnel down to the rocky seaweed-covered seabed. Of course, that was going to catch hold, because there was a seaweed-covered seabed and a good rope cable....

'Now, you coward! Catch hold of the rope,' says he, 'and run her well. The first roll that comes, hang on and maybe that will bring her out.' They were holding the rope when the first roll came and she didn't come out. She didn't succeed. When the second roll came, they were holding her and she didn't swim. When the swell went out, she fell down. The keel hit the rock and half of her went on each side and sank. That is all they got for their trouble, of the red seaweed.

I suppose that there was no luck attached to the same *púcán*. They brought her to a boatwright and they repaired her again. Now, at that time there was a good number of people dealing with poteen and selling it in shebeens. That was their misfortune and the devil as well. When they had repaired the *púcán*, they were one night inside Cuan na hAirde, that is on the lower side of Aird Mhór, which we call Cora na hAirde. There was a bad cove there, but they moored her there that evening. They were drinking poteen in the house and somebody said that it was a bad place for the boat, but nobody bothered with the boat. They didn't give the boat a second thought, but they continued to drink poteen. The following morning then, the boat was beached on the dry land and it was damaged. A section of the keel had been broken off her.

They went off with her again and they brought her to the shipwright. She was repaired. It ended up that the English police arrested them on account of the poteen and seized the boat. They brought her over to Ros Muc, up to Gleann Chatha barracks. They pulled her ashore and poured paraffin and tar on her and burnt her so that only a pile of ashes remained. That was the end of her.

37 The Kelp-test Swindle
Máirtín Ó Domhnaill, Baile Thiar, Inis Oírr

That is some years ago. Down here at the Store there was kelp being tested, and there was a man there from the government, you know. He was testing the kelp. There was a man present who had very good kelp. He broke up his sample of kelp, a little piece of his best kelp and he left some of it behind him on the flag stone. He only wanted a small piece of it to bring in to the man for testing.

He brought it in and the chemist tested it, you know, and it passed the test. When he came out, he said to the other man to gather up what he had left behind him and that it would do the trick for him to bring it in again. And he gathered up the little amount that was left over and he went in and the man inside tested it and he did not get the test at all. He did not get the price. He did not get the same price. And wasn't it a strange way, the way it was?

— Chapter Four —

DISCUSSIONS AND FIGHTING

38 Fight with Seaweed Hook — Sea Takes Cut
Strapweed Out
Máirtín Seoighe, Baile an Fhorma, Inis Oírr

I was here one day — it is forty-five years ago — and I
went down to Port na Cille. And I had my donkey there.
And by dad, when I had the seaweed was drying down there.
And there was thirty-two people out looking for seaweed
the same day. And when ... this man had a heap ... a load of
seaweed gathered up [from the sea]. And when this fellow
arrived, he just started to fill [his basket] on his horse. 'Ah,'
said one of them to him, this man said, who was this side
of him, 'I gathered that,' says he.

'If you have,' said he, 'I had it gathered already out of the
tide.'

'Well if you did, it is yours. Would you sell some to this
man?'*

But they were filling [seaweed] together, and they were
two cousins, and one of them started to ... he gave ... he
stuck the *bocán* in the seaweed. He dragged some of that
seaweed over towards himself to put in the basket. And the

---

* Translation is tentative as the original is unclear at this point.

other man asked him what he did. He said that it couldn't be helped.

All he did was ... he hit him. All he did ... to the other man ... what reason he had to do that. He just hit him with the *bocán* across there.*

He stood up. The other man was bent down and what did he gave him but a belt of the *bocán*. He hit him in the ear and by dad, when he did, they caught him and put him standing. And they made up their disagreement and went down to the shore again, filling with their horses. And when they did, it was not long till a man came over with his *bocán* in his hand.

'Where is the seaweed,' says he, 'that I had gathered?'

'That man is after filling it,' said this man.

Seeing that he had, this man just headed for him and caught him by the throat. And he shook him like a dog would a rabbit. And by dad, seeing that it was, 'Ah,' says this man, who was beside him, 'don't kill him,' says he.

But by dad, he let him off. The seaweed started to dry on the strand and every man on the beach started to gather. It was not long until every man on the beach was bringing up seaweed. Every man was by now laying into the work and they put on their sheepskins and they put their baskets on their backs and were carrying seaweed up until evening.

By dad, when evening came, the heaps were up on high ground and every man went home and put dry clothes on. And it was over on the sand they put the seaweed. And when they went down again in the evening, well if you saw the sea, didn't she rise up, up, thirty yards up and over the heaps that every man had made, that every man had gathered, and she didn't leave one 'sop' on the strand that she didn't sweep away with her.

---

* Storyteller demonstrated where.

By dad, every man came home and though every man was drenched wet, there wasn't one bit [of seaweed] to put on their fields. By dad, they went asleep that night. They got up early next morning and they didn't know what they were going to do. It was spring time then. It was the month of March. Every man went out to cut a strand of *coirleach*. And indeed that is now over forty-five years ago.

Every man started cutting, the man who had a horse, the man who had a donkey and every man; every man with a knife, cutting the *coirleach*.

I believe that every man cut anything from twenty to thirty baskets. They put it on the *dúirling*.*

Every man spread it out [to dry] in order to have it for his fields. And the next morning when they went out, the south-south-east wind was [blowing in from] the sea, and there wasn't a single heap left to anybody that wasn't swept away by the sea. And all that after their trouble, work and sweat all day. And what they said was:

'We will not get any whisp this year that will fertilise our fields.'

And that is all there is of that.

39 'Watch Out for Johnny Rankel!'
Seán Ó Conghaile, Cnoc na hAille, Indreabhán.

They had these funny stories, in olden days, you understand, when times were hard and when people had no money, when there was no dole, no meat and nothing to be got, except for 'relief'.

---

* Sometimes used as a bleaching ground.

Anyway, one day, so I heard, the people of the village were picking carrageen moss, you understand. At that time, they used to pick the carrageen in the summer in order to sell it, and often you would have to go out to the deep water, up to your waist. In those days, the old women used to make shirts from flour bags, of calico, from cotton bags as they would say. They were very good.

Well, there used to be a brand of flour that time, with a picture on the flour bag of a man holding a stick, of John Rankel, you understand, praising his own flour.

They were one day cutting seaweed or picking carrageen, and they were waiting for the tide to go out. Anyway, there was this particular woman, an old woman, and she was somewhat capricious, you understand. She was out in the sea. She hadn't the patience to wait, do you understand. She was stretching her hand down the full length of her arm, picking the weed. Someone said then, just for fun; 'How is it that we are not able to go out, as well as this woman?'

She had her clothes, the petticoat, her red coat, tied up, but her shirt was hanging down behind, and the picture of the man who had the stick raised, was to be seen on her behind.

'I will go out,' says one man or maybe it was a woman. 'I will go out along with this woman.' And the other man said; 'Oh,' says he, 'watch out for Johnny Rankel!'

40 Tough Talk at Seaweed Boundary
Ciarán Mac an Iomaire, An Cuillín, Cill Chiaráin

Pádraig Ó Conaire and Pádraig Ó Con Aola, they were cutting seaweed side by side, back in this village, in a place they call An Choarainn. Pádraig Ó Con Aola was trespassing into Pádraig Ó Conaire's patch and Pádraig Ó Conaire said to Pádraig Ó Con Aola:

'You are going across the boundary [into my weed].'

'I am not,' said he, 'I am not,' said Pádraig Ó Con Aola.

'You are,' said Pádraig Ó Conaire, 'and get out,' said Pádraig Ó Conaire, 'of my seaweed.'

'Stick your finger in my behind,' said Pádraig Ó Con Aola.

'I will let you have the pitchfork,' said Pádraig Ó Conaire.

'Stick it up in your behind,' said Pádraig Ó Con Aola, 'with the musical side sticking down.'

This happened between maybe thirty and thirty-five years ago. They were cutting black bladderweed, you know, the sort that has the fingers.

41   Jealous Man Strikes Strapwrack Cutter with Stone
Val Ó Donnchadha, Bantrach Ard, Cill Chiaráin

There are many things relating to those seaweed rafts, but they are not as plentiful now. Hardly anyone is cutting the weed for them now. Not only that, no seaweed is being cut nowadays [for fertiliser].

Anyhow, there was a man in this village and he had large plots of seaweed and he had seaweed on this particular island, strapwrack, serrated wrack, black seaweed, every kind on this division he had. And perhaps there were others in the village who had other sections.

He resented their having the strapwrack. He was a bit old, he was not a good swimmer and there was a long way to go in the channel between the island and the mainland.

There is a little harbour down here, Caladh Chorra na gCapall. Boats used be moored there, small boats and big boats at that time. And he went and took an oar and lay on it and he thought he would swim in. He was only half way when he lost his grip. He lost the oar and he lost his hat, but he managed to save his life somehow. So the strapwrack man survived, if he didn't...

But it was not long till he got revenge. He went in with a boat that was lobster fishing. They did not think he was going to do anything out of the way, or that he was rowing down beside this boat, a boat that was there.

He had a rounded stone from the storm beach in his pocket and he threw the stone and he hit a poor man who was working hard cutting seaweed [in the deep] with a crosspole. He hit him over the ear and he sent him headlong into the front hold and he half-killed him.

42 Widow Attacks Seaweed Thieves with Stones
Ciarán Mac an Iomaire, An Cuillín, Cill Chiaráin

A man and his two sons went out cutting seaweed on Mason Island. And where the devil did they go cutting it but to the shore of this old woman. She was a widow.

They were not long cutting when the old woman spotted them. She put the lower end of her skirt into her mouth and she ran to the place where they were. Her skirt was full of stones she had gathered. They were cutting the seaweed on a rock that was a distance from the island, maybe it was some hundred yards away from the island. Carraig na gCon was the name of the rock.

And this old man who was kind of odd, started using hard language with her and she was answering back and fighting with him. With that she headed out to where they were. She began to make her way through the water. The place wasn't dry, the strand wasn't dry and soon she was up to her armpits in the water and she had a long way yet to go but the place was too deep. Therefore, she turned back and the old man threw a grapnel (small anchor) that was in the boat, at her and it landed in her backside. She turned and ran as quickly as she could to save herself. Then she went to the guards and she brought a court case against him on account of it. He had to pay for it. That's all there is to the story.

— Chapter Five —

LAW AND THE COURTS

43 Court over Broken Jaw
Micheál Mac an Iomaire
An Cuillín, Carna

I am going to tell a bit of a story now about two men from Árainn. There were these two men from Árainn, about 60 years ago, and they were on the strand looking for seaweed for potato manure. And it wasn't long until one of the men spoke to the other and he said to him:

'Clear off,' said he, 'out of my seaweed, you thieving beggar,' said he, 'and don't be cutting my seaweed.'

'Well,' said the other man, says he, 'you clear off,' said he. 'I don't want any of your seaweed,' says he.

But they continued to argue with one another for a long time. Each of them had a knife, two big knives, for cutting seaweed. And the age of one of the men was ... they were both fairly old men ... but one of the men — Ó Cualáin, he was exactly four score years on this day. And the other man was one of the Conghaile. He was over three score. But Ó Cualáin was thinking Ó Conghaile was cutting his seaweed. And the thing became so serious that the two of them started hitting each other. And Ó Cualáin hit Ó Conghaile one blow and broke his jaw. Anyway, he had to be taken to the doctor and had to be sent, I believe, to hospital, because his jaw was broken.

But after about a few months, there was a court case about it and when the judge ... he asked Ó Cualáin:

'Well,' says he, 'did you break his jaw,' said he, 'with one fist?' says he to Ó Cualáin.

'Well,' says Ó Cualáin, 'your honour, I only hit him one small blow,' says he, 'and I broke his jaw.'

'Well,' says the judge, says he, 'it's a great pity,' says he, 'that you weren't trained,' says he, 'when you were a young man,' says he, ' and you wouldn't leave a man in the world,' says he, 'without breaking his jaw.'

That's all there is in the story.

44 The Judge Learns His Lesson
Cóilín Ó Cualáin, Meall Rua, Maoinis, Carna

Well, now we were talking about the strapweed (*coirleach*). The landlords were thrifty and they were hedging in a lot of the shore for themselves. The way of the shore and the seaweed had to be in accord with land of the landlord, and according as the landlord would have tenants on his own barony.

Well now, there was a lot of that going on. Then there were the bailiffs, the watchers, who the landlord had out and who used to keep a sharp eye on these people, for fear they would be cutting seaweed on the shores, or on the shore of the landlord as well. And they used to be taken and the law put on them, a fine used to be put on them. Up to a certain time, it wasn't possible (according to the law of the land) to put a fine on anybody who was out on a depth of eighteen feet cutting the strapweed with a crosspole, because it belonged to nobody.

At one time there was no (easy) means of travelling in the country except by boat. Otherwise you would have to walk by foot to Galway or to Castlebar or to any place you would want to go. There were no roads then. There was a judge who was one time going in a big boat from Roundstone to Galway. When he was sailing along the coast he saw a lot of boats with big crosspoles being pushed down into the sea and strapwrack being pulled up.

'Well,' says he to the man of the big boat, 'what are those men doing down there?'

'Well, what they are doing,' said the man of the big boat, 'they are cutting strapwrack and bringing it ashore to make kelp.'

'Well, isn't it terribly hard work what they are doing,' says he, 'pulling up that seaweed from the bottom of the sea. Or is it cut down below?' says he.

'Oh well, no,' says the man of the big boat. 'They are tearing it from the flagstones.'

'Oh isn't it terribly heavy work they have,' says he, 'do you think it pays well?' (We know that it doesn't pay. We will have a lot to say about that later.)

'Well, that's how it is,' says the owner of the big boat. 'You could say that,' says he, 'that it means a lot of hardship to them, and that they have a frightful struggle doing that.'

'Isn't what you are doing a lot worse?'

'But then what am I doing?' says the judge.

'Well,' says he, 'the next day when you come to Roundstone or Carna or over to Derrynea or anywhere there is a court of law, you will put a fine, perhaps a pound of money, on the people who are doing that work, or you will put them into prison.'

'And are those the people,' says the judge, 'that I am putting a fine on?'

'They are the same people,' says the man of the big boat.

'Well there are many, many of those cases coming to me,' says he, 'but I never knew that it was on those people that I was doing it.'

'Well let it be known to you now,' says the owner of the big boat.

So, the judge had to admit his fault. The devil a penny of a fine — good or bad — was ever put on any man who was cutting the strapwrack from then on in this place. When the judge came round again he said, 'Anybody being brought to court about seaweed that is being cut out in the sea,' says he, 'I am not going to put a fine on him.' And from then on he never fined any of these people or put a prison sentence on them.

45 Seagulls and Sods*
Ciarán Mac an Iomaire, An Cuillín, Cill Chiaráin

There was a landlord here in Carna once, maybe he did not live in Carna but nearby, who owned a rock far out in the sea, that we call Inis Múscraí. He thought that he owned all of the seaweed, the strapwrack or whatever was growing on the rock.

Anyhow at this time there were a lot of people engaged with the sea and making kelp. They were drying it and selling it for fertiliser from end to end of Ireland. A certain crowd from Leitir Mealláin came to this rock with their boats, perhaps four or five, and they went cutting the seaweed and loading it into their boats. The owner of the rock

---

* Cf. also Mac Imoire 1995, Cladai Chonamara, p.242-3.

found this out and he was going to take a fee from them, but ... but they weren't satisfied to pay it.

He brought them to law. The attorney asked them was there any grass growing on the rock and the landlord said there was. Then the landlord sent men out by night. They took sods on which the green grass was growing and they covered part of the top of the island of the top of the cliff with sods. They cut the sods on the mainland or cut them near the shore, in a place which they were growing near to the sea. They cut them with a spade and they put them in a boat and they rowed out eight or nine miles where they put them on the flagstone or on the rock which was perhaps twenty feet or more above high tide.

However, in the morning when the day was breaking the seagulls came and they took the sods with them in their claws and they threw them in the sea except for an occasional one. But before the day of court came the magistrate sent a legal official to the island to see was there any grass growing anywhere on the island or on the cliff. The official found out how the man himself (the landlord) put them there and how they were cut with a spade on the mainland and that they were brought out in a boat and they were spread over the rock. So, the case was thrown out.

It was the legal official whom the magistrate had sent out to the island that would tell the truth about it, whether there was any grass growing out on the island. The man told the truth, that never the slightest amount of grass or sod or soil was to be found on the island. There was never anything else there but the bare rock. He saw that nothing of the kind was originally there, but that some person put it there. The case was dismissed. There was no fine put on the men that cut the seaweed.

Above: Seán de Bhalís
Below left: Máirtín Ó Domhnaill
Below right: Val Ó Donnchadha

Above: Islander with bocán (seaweed hook)

Below: Gathering black seaweed

Above left: Cóilí Ó Conghaile
Above right: Mícheál Ó Donnchadha

Below left: Joe Mháirtín Uí Fhlatharta
Below right: Joe Ó Domhnaill

Above: Gathering kelp on Inis Oírr

Below: Spinning at home

Above: Heinrich Becker and Willy Ó Conghaile on Inis Oírr

Below: Giving the donkey a helping hand

There wasn't the slightest piece of seaweed cut by the landlord himself either.

That is true. It's not possible to tell half of the truth about the tyranny that was practised by some of these big bucks. They were terrible tyrants with poor people and the people who lived by the coast were poor slaves and they were trampled down by these tyrants. Probably it was long years since I heard these things, you know, but you are going to keep these things in mind always.

46 No Map, No Proof
Micheál Ó Cearbhalláin, Carna

Across the bay from Cill Chiaráin, just out from the Arramara Teoranta factory is a little island called Cinnailí. That island is cut up into parts for everyone in Cill Chiaráin or nearly everyone in Cill Chiaráin.

A man from outside of Cill Chiaráin went into that island and he gathered a great deal of seaweed. He brought it into the factory and he got paid there. Another man came and said that the seaweed didn't belong to the man who had gathered it, but to him. He said that he was going to take him to court. And then I heard that it would be coming up in the court in Carna about a year ago, maybe in the year 1973. But that matter never came to court. But it might come up yet because he was able to prove that this man was gathering on his seaweed [plot]. But as I said already he has no map. His land wasn't there — he was just saying that he had a right. Maybe he hasn't...

He had no proof. I think myself that it will be very difficult to prove that in a court in front of a Judge.

47 Case on Rambling Weed Dismissed
*Val Ó Donnchadha, Bantrach Ard,
Cill Chiaráin*

One time there was a man and he had seaweed gathered and in my opinion he was rather stubborn. Of course he was right in one way. But really the man had no right to the place. The other man came who thought he had rights and he started fighting with him and he didn't let him have the weed.

He (the 'owner') sent him a summons to bring him to court. I don't know whether he got a solicitor to take action against him.

The judge questioned what kind of seaweed was it.

'Well,' said he, the defendant, 'drifting weed.' 'It will come into the inlet with the southern wind,' says he. 'As sure as Easter is on Sunday, it's mine today, and perhaps it's yours tomorrow,' says he. 'We call it "rambling weed". It comes in here,' says he, 'it drifts in here today, out it goes again with the wind tomorrow and it comes in somewhere else.'

'Case dismissed,' said the judge.

— Chapter Six —

TRICKS AND THEFT

48 **Thief, Beggar, Murderer (A. Th. 921 B)**
Pádraig Ó Máille, Corr na Rón, Láir,
Indreabhán

There was a man who had three sons. One of the sons was a priest, one of them was a solicitor and one of them a doctor. The man owned a lot of seaweed in the place. According to the land they owned, they had a corresponding amount of seaweed, so to speak. They would have seaweed as was allotted to them in accordance with the possession of land.

At any rate, this man was well off, but his neighbours who had only small patches of seaweed were cutting the seaweed without his knowledge and stealing it as you would say, or whatever you may call it. He came upon them one day when they were cutting the seaweed. He recognised them and he summoned them so that he could bring them to court on account of cutting it.

His son was a lawyer in the place and when he got a solicitor to bring them to court, they had to go to town (Galway) so that they themselves would get a solicitor. Whom would they meet in Galway but the son. He knew very well that they were looking for a solicitor to go to court against his father. So he had a talk with them. 'I believe that you are going to take a solicitor against my father.' 'So it is,' they said. 'Well, you had better take me then,' said the son.

'Ora,' says one of them, 'why would we take you and we going to court against your father, of course, we do not think that you would work well for us.' 'Well, if you take any other solicitor,' says he, 'you will lose, but if you take me, you will win.'

'By God,' they said then to themselves that they would take his advice. They took him. This solicitor was a young man. The father then used to wear spectacles. On the day of the court the case was called and the reason put forward why the two parties were up in court. The plaintiff began to speak then, and said that he used to be keeping an eye on his seaweed and that they had been cutting it.

He had gone to the shore that day keeping guard on his seaweed and he caught these three cutting seaweed in his share. That was when his son stood up who was defending them and handed a letter or a sheet of paper to him to read. The father then put his hand in his pocket for his glasses, the spectacles as you would say. His son said to him. 'Why, can you not read it without the glasses.' — 'Oh I can not,' said the father.

'Were you wearing your glasses the day that you saw these men on the shore?'

'No, I wasn't,' said the father.

'If you weren't,' said the son, 'how can you say that they were the same men?'

So they won the case against the father. The father was very angry when he saw that his own son fought the case for them and didn't take his part at all. But the son didn't care, he was only concerned with the legal side of it.

(I believe that he was one of the Conroys of Rosmuck back in Connemara. That's what the father said then.) He went out and he was furious and he said: 'I have a son who is a liar, this is the solicitor. And I have a son who is a murderer referring to the doctor. And I have a son who is a beggar,' said he, 'the priest.' (That is the same man.) His three sons were like that, you understand, the doctor, the priest and the solicitor.

49 Laceweed Trickster Outwits Porter Trickster
Cóilí Ó Conghaile, Baile Thiar, Inis Oírr

We were over at Seán's house, one evening, to get our pay for the fish caught during the season and we had a fairly good drop drunk. And this big man — Folan was his name — he said, 'Let you be drinking,' says he, 'and I'll be ordering.'

'Very well,' said I myself. And then I thought to myself. But, by dad, it was up on twelve o'clock, surely, when we left him. And he went up home. And I myself came home, here. 'Well, now,' said I, 'it appears that he was trying to get me drunk, so that I would not go down to the shore, but I'll be a match for him.'

All I did was to bring my old oilskin with me and back I went and it was well in the middle of the night and the tide was ... the tide was just barely leaving the seaweed. And I started throwing the seaweed up on top of myself. I heard the stones rolling down from under his feet as he was coming.

'You are coming,' says I, 'and I have to think of some kind of plan.' I threw a big heap of seaweed over myself, up on me. The tide was not far from it. The tide was high enough. And the first place it came ... when he saw this pile of seaweed here, he put his two hands around it and I was inside it, inside the laceweed.

'Let me go,' said I. Oh he panicked. 'Is that you?' said he.

'It can't be that you are there.' 'It is me indeed,' says I, 'and you are late now, I have gathered up your seaweed,' said I.

And he had to go home without anything. When he saw the big heap (of seaweed), he thought that it was a lot, but what was inside it — myself and the laceweed around me.

50 The Stolen Seaweed Raft
Mícheál Ó Cearbhalláin, Carna

Now it happened also that a young lad by the name of Pádraic Dundas ... a very nice lad he was — he went ... He was cutting seaweed for the factory. The weed became scarce around Cill Chiaráin. He then went and bought weed on an island near Ros Muc. When he had cut the weed, he had made it up into a seaweed raft, and he left it on the ground as the tide was out and there was not enough water to tow it away.

He came back the following day. But while he was at home that night a certain crowd by the name of N.N., from Ros Muc and a few others, whom I do not know either, came there. They also cut weed for the factory.

They saw the raft afloat. They went then and put a lot of large stones on the raft. The raft sank because it couldn't float. It doesn't take much to sink it anyway because there is seventy per cent of it under water. A large portion of it is under water.

The raft went down and when the man came the following day, he did not see the weed anywhere and he thought it was gone. When he left then, they brought the weed into the factory. They did not go by water, but by lorry from Ros Muc.

The people who had sunk the seaweed with stones, they lifted it again and sold it to the factory. I have no proof for this, but that is the story I heard. There was no litigation involved at all.

Question: Who owned the weed?

Answer: No one, I don't think anyone was able to prove he owned it as it was on an island. It was very difficult to say who owned the weed. No one was saying that they owned it, but the people were going out and cutting it. It was happening all the time. People were going out to cut it, and probably, if there was any owner...if there was, perhaps the owner was dead, perhaps he was in America. It is difficult to say. There is a lot of weed around and no one knows who owns it. Everyone is watching that seaweed. They go and they cut that weed. Those who would do that, do not own the weed.

51 Keening Puts Greedy Seaweed-Gatherer to Flight
Pádraicín Ó Conghaile, Baile Thiar, Inis Oírr

As regards the seaweed, Willy from back there and Thomás Ó Conghaile from over here, they used to go back at midnight and stay there gathering for the night. Perhaps the whole shore would be full [of seaweed], and they would spend the night bringing it up. They resented anyone having anything, do you understand, but wanted it all for themselves. And they used to [too]. They would have a half ton brought up when the other people would arrive over.

But these lads, three or four of them, went back, having fun. They went down to the seaweed and started to keen. When Willy heard the keening, he had no idea in the world who was above [keening]. 'O, woe, woe, mammy, o woe, mammy, O ... ' they were saying, and, 'my Willy, my Willy, go home, my Willy, go home,' and so on. Willy thought that it was his [dead] mother or somebody, ordering him to go home. And Willy and Tom over here, stayed away from the beach every night from that on.

One beggar resented the other. Having got his own [share], he would not be satisfied until he had all that was on the shore. When another came, he would think that he should get nothing, do you understand.

52 'The Sheet Has Not Been Wetted Yet Beside Them'
Seán Ó Conghaile, Cnoc na hAille, Indreabhán

Well, it's about forty years ago since I heard the following story, you understand, when seaweed was being used as fertilizer. It was very important and it was well minded by them. They wouldn't let the smallest amount of it go to waste. It was the red weed here which mattered, that is to say, the kind which comes in with the tide. *Bruth fá thír* is what some people call it. Wreckweed, do you know. The gale tears it off and it drifts ashore. This now was in April and at that time the weed was very important for tillage.

There were two old men one evening over in Spiddal and they were ... talking with one another. They were from the area. They saw the nice strip of seaweed coming in with a big wave and they said, 'We will be up early in the morning now and collect that.'

Do you know, the first person that would come would have the seaweed. Nobody had any claim to it, except he who would be there first. It was very important, then, do you know, for spreading on the land.

They said that both of them would get up early, which they did. It was Monday morning. They were there at around four or five in the morning. However, two young lads were there before them collecting the seaweed and once you would lay your hands on it, it is yours. Nobody else could take it from you. That was the law, at the time.

The two old men stood and looked down on the two young lads gathering the weed and one of them said to the other, 'Well,' says he, 'the sheet has not yet been wetted beside them in the bed, but when it will be, they will stay asleep in the morning.'

That meant in olden times the man and the woman slept together with the child in between them. When the child would pass water, as you would say, the sheet would be wet. Now that is a story which I heard.

53 Clever Servant Boy Tricks Greedy Master
Pádraig Mac Donnchadha, Ros a'Mhíl

It's about ... it's a long time since it happened. What name do I call him at all? This man was back there in Cillín, in a place called Barr an Doire, down from An Cheathrú Rua.

There was a man there and he had a [servant]-boy. Well, he wanted every bit of the seaweed for himself and to leave none for anybody else.

He would send the boy out at night long before day, so that he would have the seaweed gathered. Gathering red seaweed they were. But he sent the boy out before himself. The boy went off, and he himself went to some other place, so that they would have every place when it would be day. And the boy heard the master coming and what did he do but stretch himself out, and throw all the seaweed he had gathered over himself. And the master came and saw the seaweed. 'Upon my soul, there is seaweed gathered, good seaweed here,' says he. He went off himself to gather more. And the boy was wearing a new pair of shoes.

'By dad,' says he, 'there are new shoes on the drowned man,' says he, 'by dad, I will take them off him.' Anyhow, he was taking off the shoes and when he had one shoe taken off, the boy pulled the other shoe and hit him here in the chest.* And he landed him on the beach. And when he got up ... this was back in Barr an Doire. Yes, he hit him in the chest with the other foot, with the other shoe.

When he got up he ran and left the shoe he had taken off behind as well. And all the boy did was to put on the other shoe again.

And the man was waiting for him and asked the boy 'Did you gather seaweed?' 'I gathered some,' said the boy, 'did you gather much yourself?' 'I didn't gather any,' says he. 'I've had enough. I won't go gathering any seaweed again as long as I live,' says he. 'I found a drowned man,' says he, 'and he gave me a blow,' says he, 'after being drowned,' says he, 'and I won't be seen on the beach any more.'

---

* Storyteller points at his chest.

A woman from the same place was telling this, from the place, from Cillín. The woman was from Cillín and the two men were from Cillín. She knew them well, she did.

54 Two Lobsters as Bribe (Kelp Test)
Val Ó Donnchadha, Bantrach Ard, Cill Chiaráin

It was my father himself who told it to me. When he was a young man, he used to go lobster fishing, he himself and a relation of his from Aird Mhóir. Anyway there were going out at the beginning of summer and they prepared a little kiln of kelp.

They had every kind of seaweed in the kelp. They had every kind of seaweed. They had drifted weed,* channel wrack, they had black bladder seaweed, they had stranded drift weed and every kind and drift weed mixed up. Anyhow they made the kiln. They used drift weed that came ashore. But when they had the kiln mixed and had got it ready, it was only half a foot high, it was as thin as pancake.

All the same, they took it back to Cill Chiaráin and it was Mr Hazel who was living in Caiseal, it was he who was in charge of the kelp. There was a man before him in Cill Chiaráin who was an agent of his whom they called Pat Dick; he was a Mac Donnchadha. Anyhow on this day when they were going over to the eastside, they had put out some lobster pots and they had caught lobsters. And one man of them took two lobsters out of a few collecting pots, an extra pot they had.

---

* *Himanthalia lorea*

Anyhow they took the two lobsters with them out of the extra pot and took them with them. But when they went over, one of them went up to the house of Pat Dick bringing the two lobsters with him which were wrapped up in an old homespun jacket and he said to the woman of the house, 'Here,' said he, 'are two lobsters,' said he, 'which I brought along,' said he, 'for Mr Hazel's dinner.' She thanked him and when she told that — as I believe — to the gentleman (I may as well call him such), he thanked her very much.

We used to call him Mr Hazel, but I don't know if he had any land, for a while. — Yes! Oh, he owned the whole district, he was the heir to the district, all this once was the Scannell estate. And Lynch, too, was once an heir to an estate. He was the heir to the district accordingly. Colonel Martin was the heir to the district in Baile na hInse for some time.

'Anyway,' he said, Hazel said to Pat Dick, 'Well,' said he, 'you will weigh whatever amount of kelp they have in that pile,' says he, 'weigh it for them,' says he, 'they don't need any test,' says he, 'it is tested already.' —Well, when he came with the kelp, they put it out. Everybody was looking at it, they were a sort of ashamed. It was looking so miserable. It was thin and it was in every state.

Anyhow, the wall of the quay, the wall of the quay, stretching along out on the pier ... it was weighed then and put into the storehouse in the form of tremendously big stone blocks. Some of those stone slabs used to weigh five hundredweight, and four hundred pounds and so on.

— Chapter Seven —

THE LIVING DEAD AND THE FAIRY HOST

55 **Dead Sailor's Thanks for Burial**
*Val Mac Donnchadha, Bantrach Ard,
Cill Chiaráin*

There were two other women over in Leitir Mealláin and they
used to be picking dulse on Oileán an Arma, an island lying
east of Gólam Head, south of Leitir Mealláin. They call it
Oileán an Arma. Girls used to stay there overnight on bright
moonlit nights to gather dulse. They had a shelter there.

Anyhow, two girls were staying on the island this particular night and they went down to pick a night-strand of dulse
while the bright moon was out. On their way back from
below they came across a sailor, at least that's what they
thought he was, drowned, among the drift.* They took a look
at him as they thought they might as well do that much.

'What do you think at all,' says one of them to the other,
'we should do with him?' 'Ah, I don't know,' says the other,
'but wouldn't it be better for us … there's a kind of sand
bank up on the island. Whoever he is,' says she, 'or whatever
his religion might be, we'll go down on our knees and say a
prayer for his soul. Maybe that's the best thing we could do.'

---

* *Snáth mara* (thus Ó *Dónaill*) = high-water line formed of wrack and other
matter drifted ashore.

And so they did. And between the two of them they carried him up, made a hole, put him in it and covered him. Then they went down on their knees again and said a prayer for him. They did.

After that they went to their hut and ate a kind of supper. They were chatting away and conversing and just when they were about to go to sleep, he came, the man they had buried. He came and stood outside in front of the door. Of course, the poor creatures nearly fainted.

'Ah,' says he, 'don't be scared. I won't do anything to you. But let you be thankful,' he said 'for your good-heartedness and for your prayers. This was my last night on earth,' says he, 'but don't be afraid; there is no danger for you. I am going to leave you now.' And off he went.

But at dawn they lit a signal fire and were taken off [the island]. And not a soul ever stayed there overnight again.

56 Dead Woman Assists Seaweed-Gatherer
Val Ó Donnchadha, Bantrach Ard, Cill Chiaráin

Long ago, people used to put up red weed on the strand of Iorras Mór. Everyone of them had a horse, a straddle and baskets and a tying rope. They had the straddle and the straw mat fixed up and a strap on each side. Then there is a rope tied to each basket which we call the tying rope. When the seaweed has been filled, the ropes are tied. One man is able to load seaweed well and another not so well. But the man I am talking about, there was no one as good as him at all to fill a load of seaweed.

I heard before that, he used to see a woman who had left the world, a relation of his own. He no more feared her than if she were alive. He used to see her when he went out at night. She used to walk with him and so on.

This man was putting up the seaweed and he got some word that his wife at home or one of the children ... that someone was sick, and he left the horse there, standing on the shore. The horse did not move. There were three or four other men there and they thought they would do well, that they would have so many loads of seaweed up, before he came back.

This woman did not like it. They didn't see the woman, but she was there, for sure. Only for she was [they would have done that thing]. They failed to bring up any load of seaweed. When he came back, he saw her and he spoke to her, but they did not see her. 'Ah,' she says, 'they are at work, trying to work hard ever since, trying to get the better of you, [to bring] so many loads of seaweed up, but they didn't put up a wisp since you left and I did not let them,' says she. 'Every load they filled,' says she, 'I used to stick a searod in the horses' backsides and they were knocking the loads and they didn't succeed.' 'Thank you very much,' he says, and he started to cry when he knew it.

But, you know, there was a lot of that happening long ago, or so it was said. But what they say concerning that, man or woman, that they did not leave this world at all, but they underwent a change of existence. Ara, I tell you now, there are a thousand and a hundred things about them, if you and I had the time to give them to you.

57 Spirit Advises Against Seaweed Theft
Cóilín Ó Cualáin, Meall Rua, Maoinis, Carna

Long ago, in olden times here, well it is not all that long ago, the man who told me this little story was a young lad.

They used to have a great time on St Patrick's Day in these areas around here. The pubs are not ... they were not open at all. They were kept closed by law at the time.

What they mostly availed of, so to speak, was the shebeen. They would go to the shebeen house and get a pint or two of poteen.

The money was very scarce and a certain old man said to me — God be good to his soul — that the plan he and another young man thought of a few days before St Patrick's Day was to go ... there were old women at the time, and old people, and they had a little money, and if you could cut a boatload of seaweed for them, they would pay you for it.

This man said, 'There was a spring tide,' says he, 'and a fine tide it was and a fine moon and the weather was very good. This other man and I said to one another,' says he, 'that we would go into Inis Bigir and that we would go into weed belonging to a man there, a man from Maoras — he owned the whole place at the time — that we would go in and cut a boatload and we would bring it to this old woman, and we would have enough money for St Patrick's Day.'

They got the boat ready and off they went and they came ashore where the weed was. 'And the tide was going out and going out fast,' he says. The first man went out and brought with him the rope and fastened it. When the two got out and began cutting, a man walked down to them and he said to them, 'You would be better off going elsewhere, and leave it alone.' They left the seaweed behind them and went home. It was someone who had left this world, I suppose. He was probably saving the weed for the living owner, on this earth.

Is it not laid down for us that the dead are able to do good to us, but that they are unable to do any good at all for themselves. Did you ever hear that?

Answer: No, I didn't.

Indeed they are. They say that if you are paying for the dead, saying prayers for them and praying for them in your own way, they are able to do you good. But they will not do themselves any good, they are not able to do themselves any good.

Well, there is another thing [too]; there was a lot of magic in these matters. I will tell you another little story...

58 The Fairies Punish Nocturnal Seaweed Gatherer
Seán Ó Conghaile, Scoil Náisiúnta Inis Meáin, Ceathrú an Teampaill, Inis Meáin

There was a man long ago and he went over to the Slip to gather seaweed. The fairies, they brought him down into the rockpool and they were beating him with searods. They dragged him up and down the rockpool and he was drenched wet. The fairies left then and the man got up.

He went up the Slip and as he was going back by Carcair Dáibhí he heard a noise behind him. He saw a white ass going into the cliff. The same man was coming up Muirbheach Trá Leitreach and he heard a noise. He looked and saw a fairy behind him. He went into the house and he shut the door tightly and went to sleep. When he got up in the morning, the dog was dead at the door.

59 Sabbath Seaweed Gatherers Penalised by Ghostly Beings
Pheadaí Ó Conghaile, Baile an Chaisleáin, Inis Oírr

It was a Saturday night and we went back to the shore and, by gor, when we arrived there was seaweed to be gathered there. There were four of us there, myself and my brother, and two other brothers. The four of us were working together. By gor, we gathered it into baskets, and put it on the bank, trying to keep it clear of the tide, we were putting it on the storm beach. The sea was running high, but it was ebbing, do you understand? It had to be gathered [the seaweed] and we were all alone.

By gor, when I had spent some time gathering, I came up with a basket and I was swept out to my waist, out into a lot of water, carrying the basket. It was as heavy as two hundredweight, and no man there could carry such a basket as I carried then. 'Ara,' one of the others asked, 'did you fill the basket with sand?'

'No,' I replied, 'The empty basket had been filled with sand while it was on the rock.' And if so, 'I did not do it;' said I.

But we brought in the second basket then and I went waist deep in the pool and by gor I brought in as much as forty basket-loads to the shore. Two of us were engaged in gathering, the other two were filling the baskets. We brought the seaweed ashore. I brought as much as four or five score baskets ashore, and when I returned to the sea around one o'clock at night, searods as plentiful as sand were coming from the cliff; they were being pelted at us. It was a Sunday night, do you understand?

Around one o'clock, or two o'clock, on Sunday night we noticed ... when we were finished working on that shore, and when we had gone to another shore, we saw a man when we went out. We did not recognise him, but he was in the sea, gathering seaweed like us. We were also gathering. We carried another load to the top of the cliff there, searods and seaweed, nearly as much as ... as much as four or five score baskets because we had spent the whole night working with it, bringing it up to the cliff. And, by gor, while we were doing that, the other man was working, gathering below us and when we had finished in that location we had amassed a fine heap of seaweed containing searods and every kind of seaweed.

Ara, it was a dead person who was throwing the searods, it wasn't a living person. 'It is the lads who are up there who are throwing down the searods,' one of them said to me. We went to a further shore and when we did so, the man was there before us. Just as we were gathering seaweed, so was he. We didn't see him properly and we couldn't recognise him.

But, by gor, we carried another load ashore, up to the top of the cliff. We weren't wearing socks or shoes. We had taken them off, we were going up the rock barefooted. The place was very slippery, if you were not [careful] ... It was a moonlight night, we had a lantern, and we made a path of sand to the place where we were leaving the seaweed.

But it soon began to brighten and we didn't see the man who was collecting, we saw nothing. The sea swelled, the sea rose in a great mass. We saw nothing of all the seaweed we had collected during the night. The sea had swept it away.

That is all we had from the night's work. We returned home exhausted.

60 Ghostboat Appears After Seaweed Theft
Val Ó Donnchadha, Bantrach Ard,
Cill Chiaráin

I myself used to be long ago ... when I was a young man and my two brothers ... One of them is still alive over in America, in Chicago — Pádraic — and then the other brother Máirtín, God rest his soul, he wasn't even a year in America when he got killed by a car. And another neighbour up here above — Cóilín Conaola, he was a close relative of ours. The four of us used to go out during the nights around the festival of Saints Peter and Paul, beyond Oileáin Bhéarra, to a place we call Maidhm na mBraems. We used to be killing breams there at night. We used to kill them — a good number of them, and other boats there apart from ourselves.

But this night the four of us went ... the night had a bad hue ... the four of us went in a rowing boat, with our oars out to Maidhm na mBraems. We started fishing for breams, but we didn't kill many. The night came bad. A storm came in from the east with rain and the rope broke. And at that time there was a bailiff on the island — Beartlaín Ó Clochartaigh and his family — and he saw us going out. He was expecting us back, but we didn't come back. But we reached the place below the house, at the mouth of the shore. And we came ashore and found it hard enough for four strokes. We were brave and spirited then. We fixed up the boat with a few ropes and my brother went out ... we put the oars across the front hold.

There were a lot of cocks of dried seaweed there in a place they call Meall an Chalaidh. There is a sort of pier there. There are huge cliffs there ... a high cliff called Meall an Chalaidh. And we put the oars across the front hold in the rowing boat to make a tent and my brother Pádraic went out, the man who is over in America now, and he filled the boat with heather, I am as well to call it heather, and he covered the oars above them with seaweed, and we lay back and started to talk and laugh and pass the night. The bailiff's house was near enough to us, but we did not go up. He was expecting us in. But between everything, I fell asleep myself. The cold wakened me and when the four of us were out in front — the rain was pouring down — and the water was going into my mouth and ears and I sat up. The day was dawning, but it was dark enough. There is an island in front of us now, called Inis Múscraí. There's another rock outside that, called Carraig na Meacan. But when we sat up, one of us said anyway,

'I wonder is that the rock out there?'

'How would you see the rock when you can't see your hand, it's so dark?' said one of us. 'It's not the rock.'

But it wasn't long till a light was lit. 'There's a light,' said one of us and when that light was lit, a light shone over from Ceann Gólaim, and a light over from Sceirde and the three of them met. And two rows of light were lit to our side, like a liner, and she turned and headed for us. We couldn't see the light very well, just the shine when it was facing us.

But we said to one another that it wasn't a place for us to be. We pulled up. We threw down the tent. We headed for home and when we were going up at a place called Bealach Charraig na Cuislean, Pádraic said,

'We must land on this rock here,' he says, 'I am carried away with fear.' It (the liner) was getting closer to us. It was so far in on the shallow part that not even a canvas currach would not float there. The biggest boat you ever saw ... noise, music and ruction ... But it was myself that spoke,

'That is not a right steamer,' says I, 'that is some kind of devil,' says I, 'that is trying to drown us.' And the word wasn't out of my mouth when she turned just like a top and headed for the open sea. She was as bright as snow and she headed off behind the island and we never saw her again. And when we came over we thought we'd see her going over outside the point, but we didn't. But I saw that much because of that night.

61 Fairies Fighting During Kelp Burning
Cóilí Ó Conghaile, Baile Thuas, Inis Oírr

We were burning kelp one night, and we were all very tired, and we spent twenty-four hours at the kiln. And when we did, went over near the stack to take a rest and I was about to throw an armful of seaweed on me thinking that I may fall asleep and have a rest. Just when I was about to lie down, it appeared to me that I heard a voice, a good bit away from me and I listened for a while that I might be sure of the voice. A man came over to the stack to get an armful of seaweed to put on the kiln. It was blazing, a huge fire. 'Listen,' I said to him, 'do you hear anything.' 'I don't hear anything,' he said. 'Listen a while,' said I, because the kiln was making such noise.

The rods and the seaweed were bursting. He stood up. 'Ah, I hear it,' he said. He went over then to the kiln, and then threw the armful he had from him, and he spoke to the crowd that was at the kiln. 'Do you hear anything?'

Everybody listened and they were looking. And the fight and the beating was going on. We did not see anybody, but we knew that they were arguing and beating each other, and that there were lots of people there. Everybody began to listen and they had a handful of seaweed in each hand and you would think that were intending to go on board a train. It looked like two bags they had in their hands in which their clothes were, they would have ... And the fire began to blaze and there was nobody putting a sop of seaweed on the kiln and I was afraid when I was looking, I was afraid that the kiln would go out without seaweed. There was no talk about putting a sop on the kiln. They were listening. In the end, I shouted, 'Don't let the kiln go down altogether, or it will go out on you.' And that was the time they started to put weed on it again, and when I looked over at the people that were over there, the blaze and the fire were, shining into their faces. Well. their faces were as white as snow in the middle of the night. And the voice was going moving away, and you'd barely hear it in the end.

But we were thinking that there were two crowds that were not on the best of terms ... as was usual, arguing with each other. But we were thinking that they were not people of this world. Whatever was between them, I think that will do now. 'Well, it is true.' Well, I did not recognise them right, but I thought that I recognised one man's voice and I should know that he was not of this world, and that is why I thought something came between them. But they went off across the crags and that is the end of my story. It is not a story with a lie.

I was there and I was listening, Edward was there too. He was, and two or three more, there were four or five others there anyway. If they were gone out of this world itself, maybe something comes between them and the people who are living themselves. They fight well, perhaps they are the same way in the other world. I don't know where they are, or where we will go, but with God's help we won't be too bad. Do you believe that there are fairies?

62 Fairies Gathering Seaweed at Sunset
Máirtín Seoighe, Baile an Fhorma, Inis Oírr

Well, of course, I will tell you. At sunset a brother of mine, he is in England now, went back here to get a can of porter, back, you know where Thomás Conghaile lives. Well, at that time it was the old people who owned it. He left the village here, there was a young lad with him. He went off at sunset. The sun was set when he left the house. He was not afraid, nor anything like that. When he came to the beach, every man in the island was gathering seaweed.

Night had fallen. There wasn't a man at that time who did not have a horse. It seemed to him as if the islanders were gathering weed. One man bringing up his load, another filling and another fixing it on the donkey. By dad, the little lad was with him. The little lad didn't see anything. He asked the little lad: 'Do you see anything?' 'I do not,' says he. 'Oh,' said he, 'do you not see the people there?' 'I do not,' says the young lad.

Back he went and got the porter, and came back the same way and there was not a man, woman or child to be seen in any place until he got home. And isn't that an amazing thing? You would hardly believe that there was anything moving about at that time, but the beach had been full of people. It was so. That is the truth. They were gathering seaweed with horses and putting it out on the fields. Well, they were people from this world who had left this life. Yes, they were people who left us.

Question: What did they do with the seaweed?

Answer: They were going to put it out on the fields. But there was nothing to be seen in any field the following morning.

63 Seaweed Sprite Diverts Fairies
Val Ó Donnchadha, Bantrach Ard, Cill Chiaráin

There was a man around here long ago, Mícheál Ó Mainnín was his name, and it was said and believed by the neighbours that he used to be going with the good people, the fairies.

He was one day at the shore, over in Doire Iorrais. He and his son, cutting yellow weed, gathering it into heaps so as to put it up with their backs and baskets, for potato fertiliser. They had to gather it into heaps and make a raised platform then and put the basket on it and put the seaweed into the basket, and the son putting his shoulder into the strap and it being raised up onto him — a fine strong young man. He had to go up across the shore and throw it up on the grass and when that was done and that strand finished until the next day. It was yellow weed that was being gathered. The place is too gentle. It is too far from the wild places and there are no currents there — gentle mud inlets and only yellow weed grows there. No one-stemmed weed grows there nor strapwrack nor anything like that. It is too far up into the land.

On this particular day Mícheál Ó Mainnín was on the shore cutting yellow weed, he and his son. And a whirlwind came. It began to lift the seaweed up and take it away and the father was looking at the son and the son was looking at him. The father was trying to do something behind his back.

These people (fairies) were putting the seaweed ... so as to spoil the seaweed on him. The son was suspicious of his father, and his father did not want him to see it. Rather than lose all the seaweed, he took up a tuft of weed and he threw it out on the sea. And the whirlwind and the storm vanished. 'Why did you do that?' said the son to the father. 'Ah, don't bother with that,' said the father. 'It is alright, let that much pass now, please.'

'I will not,' says the son, 'because I have heard it from the mouth of every authority,' says he, 'and from my neighbours, that you are going with the fairies,' says he. 'And that that is your usual practice and I must find out whether you are or not.'

'Ah, if that is so,' says the father.

'You won't leave this strand,' says the son, 'if you don't tell me.'

'Rather than you drown me, I will tell you,' says the father.

'They are now the good people,' says the father, 'I saw them well. The hills are black with them and the valleys are speckled with them, men and women. And they are taking a fine young man, from Joyce country, a young boy with a red head of hair. They have him. I saw him with my two eyes, and if you don't believe me,' says he, 'there is a lake out there, out beyond the bog of Cuilinn, Loch a' Bhuí, and his double is left on the shore of the lake on a sandy beach, and he is lying on his face frothing. And if you wish,' says he, 'to believe me, you can go out to see him with your own two eyes.'

'All right,' says the son. He put on two shoes, he turned up his pants or his drawers, if he had it on, beyond his knees, and he went out across the bog. When he came to Loch a' Bhuí, he saw a young man, red hair, lying on his face and frothing, at the top of the strand.

'Oh, the Cross of Christ on us,' says he, 'it is very bad. What is wrong with my father at all, that he can see these things or do them? And he said to me, that saw that young man with them (fairies) with his own two eyes, and I am seeing it now, but it is not he who is here,' says he. 'But I will not do him a day's service ever again.'

64 Girl Dances to Fairy Music and is Spirited Away
Seán de Bhailís, Sruthán, Inis Mór

There was a girl back at Cora Phort Uí Sheáin gathering seaweed. Her father said to her to start bringing the seaweed up from the tide and she did. And she had twenty baskets up, when the malicious music started inside the cliff. It seemed like grand music to her.

She started to dance and nothing would stop her dancing till her father came up from the shore and caught her and she stopped. He went home, she was brought home to her people. She went to bed and never left it until she died.

— Chapter Eight —

ABOUT DEMONS AND DEVILS

65 Big Walsh Kills Ghost with Black-handled Knife

Val Ó Donnchadha, Bantrach Ard, Cill Chiaráin.

There was a man here in Connemara in the old days. I can't say whether he lived in Ros Muc or in Camus. Anyhow, he had a big boat. He used to trade, bringing seaweed to the Burren and also turf to Galway. They held the opinion that he was an excellent man. There was nothing that could scare him. He was an excellent man, a fine strong man.

He had a certain customer who lived a good distance to the east of him. He thought he would meet him on a certain day to give him the seaweed and to settle matters with him. But he did not.

It wouldn't be good to leave the boat in the harbour, in at the pier, because the tide was in and if he hadn't unloaded the seaweed by the time it ebbed he would be delayed, stranded, until she floated again.

'Well,' says he to the boatman, 'I must go to that man who buys the seaweed from me. Because if we miss the tide in the morning, we will lose two, or maybe three, days. Perhaps we will unload it early in the morning and I and he will come back here. In any case, mind the boat well. And you can wait in the boat until I come back, whether it be early or late.'

He went off. However, there was a place between him and his destination called Bearna na Carcaire (The Gap of the Stump). I suppose there was a large stump of bog-deal, or something similar, there and that it derived its name from it.

It was said that a ghost was often seen there and nobody felt like going there when it was late, until he had daylight. Some people had been killed there.

Anyhow, Walsh departed and when he was coming close to Bearna na Carcaire, he saw in the middle of the road the ghost, through whose legs the whole world could pass. And Walsh shouted:

'Go on one side, boy,' says he. He paid no attention to him, but he was stooping down towards him ... It wasn't fear of the ghost that was perturbing him but he was getting a horrible stench from him which was nearly knocking him out. But finally, he put his hand in his pocket and he pulled out a knife which he had for the occasion — I suppose they were often after him — he pulled out the black-handled knife and stabbed the ghost and it collapsed as a useless heap.

He set off again and made for the house where he was going.

It was late enough. The road was long. When he arrived at the house, he knocked at the door, but the household was asleep except the girl who was cleaning the house. She called the man of the house.

'There is somebody at the door,' says she.

'Ah,' says he, 'nobody could be there this late and it could only be Big Walsh from Connemara. He wants to have his boat emptied by the morning tide. Open the door and let the poor man in.'

He was standing outside with his back turned to the door and when the girl opened the door, he fell in backwards into the middle of the floor and was completely unconscious.

The man of the house got up and they put old butter in his mouth and did everything possible — but Walsh did not regain consciousness until the cock crowed. He sat up straight.

'Oh, God save us!' says he, 'I have missed the tide and the boat is on the dry, however fares it with the boatman.'

'Oh what happened to you?' says the man from that place, 'or how did you go through the Gap of the Stump?'

'Oh, I have seen enough,' says he. 'He was there. He was as tall as the world and I wasn't afraid, I can't be scared at all, but the smell I was getting was knocking me out. I stabbed him with the black-handled knife and he fell as a useless heap in the middle of the road, and I think that the knife is still in him, but I won't leave my knife in him. With God's help when we are going back [I will get it].

They got ready and they were coming back and when they came to the spot there was a lump of slime in the middle of the road and the knife was quivering in its middle. Walsh bent down, took the knife, cleaned it and put it in his pocket. Nobody was killed, nor nobody died ever since then on account of the ghost that was in the Gap of the Stump.

He unloaded the seaweed. He unloaded it on the pier, when the owner came. They unloaded the seaweed. The owner came with a horse and cart and they unloaded the seaweed and he paid its price, big or small, and he brought it home.

That man always bought seaweed from him, for himself, or maybe, to sell it to the neighbours when he [Walsh] used to go there. Carts of the big type, those of the old big kind. A big horse drawing it over there. We used to call it the

Munster Land, but it wasn't [really] Munster Land, but in Connemara they used to call it by that name when they went east there from home. But it is not part of the Munster Land.

Some of it was for himself, for fertilising potatoes and the like. Then they used to buy oarweed, black seaweed and every sort of seaweed, [including] knotted wrack, from the Connemara people, in spring usually; black seaweed which we call one-stemmed seaweed.

[It grows] in the muddy quiet creek. But where there are channels in the sea, where there is a continuous current, the seaweed is cleaner and stronger. On account of the current, it is always kept clean.

But it doesn't grow that good where the mud and quietness are. Knotted wrack grows there.

66 Storm-witches Try to Drown Big Walsh
Val Ó Donnchadha, Bantrach Ard, Cill Chiaráin

This story is true, even if it is a ghost story, it happened, because there was proof, for the man who saw it and who performed the act. He has passed away now, God rest his soul. Fairy women, certainly, women who had left this life, who were dead or else women who were not natural.

This man, who I was talking to you about, earlier on, I don't know if he was from Camas or Ros Muc. He had a big boat and he used to trade seaweed from Kinvara to Ballyvaughan and to the Burren, as the opportunity arose. And that is the man, who I was telling you about, who killed the ghost in Bearna na Carcaire, and took with him the knife.

Some time after that, he was heading down Aill an Aráin Bay, this side of Leitir Calaidh, and there was a good breeze from the north. It was evening and he was on his own. At any rate, he glanced up and saw the ugliest hag he had ever seen, up on the deck, and she messing with the halyard, the jib halyard.

He cautioned her but she paid him little heed. There was another one with her and she was releasing the halyards ... from the cleat which was tied to the mast, trying to let the sail down. He let a roar, 'You cursed hag,' says he, 'are you hoping to drown me?' And he ran up and the one that was at the front sail or the jib, she ran out on the bowsprit. Between life and death, he put a hand in his pocket, opened his knife, threw it, and stuck the knife in the back of her neck. She let a poisonous scream and before she fell in the sea, the other one ... had taken her in her arms, between heaven and earth, and she wailing, 'May you be seven times worse off a year from tonight,' says she, 'wicked Big Walsh,' says she, 'for you have killed my poor sister.' He never saw them again.

Question: What were they?

Answer: He thought they were people who had left this life or cursed spirits. But for there was something ... they had nothing to do with this world. But for that, they wouldn't have been able to do that.

Question: Fairy women?

Answer: O maybe, fairy women, fairy women, ghosts, spirits.

67

Cursing the Gale Saves Seaweed Boat
Peadar Seoighe, Baile an Fhorma, Inis Oírr.

We had two brothers back in Cill Rónáin and the creatures had a boat. Well, you know, many other people had boats as well. And these boat people, in Spring, in March or April, used to be going out to Oileán na Tuí, over at the Cois, gathering black seaweed and strapwrack.

These boats, they were about five or six tons, they would carry five or six tons. Turf boats, we used to call them, do you understand, which used to draw turf from Connemara. You could let her in on land at half-ebb, and be cutting away, and fill the boat. Then when the tide would come in, she would swim out again.

But most of the seaweed around the village, Barr an Phointe and Oileán na Tuí had been cut. These two brothers said, 'Ah, if we were to hit back to Oileán Aerach, we would surely get a boatload of strapwrack. And we would get great money for it in Kinvara.' There's nothing wrong with that,' says Seán. 'Off with us then,' says Taimín.

They got up in the morning and back they went and of course there was a grand tide ebbing back underneath the cliffs. They went back. They had another thing in Cill Rónáin and in Connemara, to cut the strapwrack — a *croisín* [a crosspole] they called it. You'd put down this pole and you'd be tugging and tugging and you'd bring up so much each time. You'd be breaking the roots [down below].

I'm loathe to tell a lie, but I'm not sure if they let the boat in on land or kept her afloat, but at any rate, they filled her with seaweed. And on their way home, the eastern sky started to look bad. It darkened as if there were snow over Black Head and the wind shifted north eastwards and the poor man was tacking it back under the cliff.

'Well,' says Taimín to Seán, 'we'll get enough of her. Even the sea is swelling.' 'Well, I always heard,' says Seán, 'when you'd be in a boat like this and the gale and the sea making for you, if you went out front and started to curse the gale ... prayers were no good,' says he. 'You had better start cursing, until the gale passes.' 'Muise, anything that will do a person good,' says poor Taimín, 'if you like to, do it.' Out went Seán. 'Muise,' says he, 'a proper bad end to you, gale and shower,' says he, 'and may the devil and the demon and all the devils of hell take you away from us somehow.'

But when Seán spoke, by the Book, the day seemed to improve. But the creatures struggled over and when they came to ... they were coming in St Gregory's Sound, the wind had pulled westwards and after that it shifted south eastwardly. 'Well,' says Tam to Seán, 'we'd nearly tack it over to Spiddal now.' 'Ara, wouldn't I be better letting her towards Kinvara altogether, to see would we get the price of a few sacks of meal for the load of seaweed.'

Because, that time in Kinvara, when you'd go over with a load of seaweed, the farmers used to come down every morning, to see if there were any boats from Connemara or Árainn there. They were grateful to get it to buy, because I'm telling you, there was little or none of this guano coming from the wild countries that time. And the farmer liked to put some seaweed through his own manure. He would say that he could get a great crop from the field when he had the two mixed together. But they went to Kinvara and they sold the weed.

68 Black Merman Tries to Board Boat
Val Ó Donnchadha, Bantrach Ard, Cill Chiaráin

Two men from An Aird, they went to Kinvara once with a load of seaweed. People from Connemara used to go there usually with seaweed. Sometimes they would get paid for the seaweed and sometimes maybe they would get potatoes, as seeds or very often to eat. Times were bad and there wasn't a great price to be got for anything, only a little.

But these two men, when they sold this seaweed, they were heading for home, and the man who was with the man who was steering, he was sitting at the head of the stern seat with his head leaning on the weatherboard — asleep.

And when they were coming over the other side of Ceann Gólaim, out past Túr an Arma* the man who was steering heard a noise in the flow behind the boat, and he looked behind him and there was a black man, as black as the coal, holding on to the two bollards with his two big hands, trying to come aboard. He attempted to put his foot in the steering control, to come in. But the man in the boat he cried, 'Oh you devil, don't come any closer to me.' He threw himself back on his back and sunk.

They were heading west and when they were coming up beside Carraig an Iolra, it wasn't quite yet night. The place was full of people, the dark of the hills and the bright of the glens, talking and shouting and fighting, and quarrelling and contending with each other. And he was struck by

---

* This name is unclear.

terror, and great fear.* But the man who was asleep on the seat, he could not wake.

But I forgot to tell you that he was so scared that he put the crosspole in the steering wheel and that he himself stood up above the stern with fear. But when he turned over at Carraig an Iolra he had enough heard but your man did not awake. 'Ah, by Pete's,' says he, 'it must be that you are very tired.'

And he took hold of the rudder, and you know there is a good weight in the rudder of a turf boat, and he drew and hit the man in against the hip. And he didn't mean [to hurt him] ... but it was all the same, he did not wake. 'Ah, by dad,' says he, 'it must be,' says he, 'that there is some misfortune on you,' says he, 'and that this is not a natural sleep.'

He was snoring away. And when they were going up Cuan na hAirde, the poor man who was hit from behind, straightened up. He let a cry. 'Ah God and the Holy Virgin,' says he, 'my hip joint.' 'Oh, indeed, you poor thing,' says the other man, 'it is no wonder,' says he. 'You have good reason but it cannot be helped now.'

And the poor man did not walk again, but was on crutches until he died. That is my story now as I heard it.

69 Seaweeder Sees Mermaid
Seosamh Ó Flatharta, Baile an Chaisleán, Inis Oírr

Question: Talking about the mermaid, did you not see her yourself?

---

* Speaker uses the adjective '*ábhal*' in the sense of a noun, to mean great fear.

Storyteller: I did, indeed. That's not much [of a story].

Woman of the house: Indeed, it's not much of a story.

Question: Where did you see her?

Storyteller: Here, below.

Question: What were you doing below?

Storyteller: Well, I got up at dawn early in the morning and I went down to Port na Cille. That was all right. I stood up straight. The tide was high ... no, the tide was not high. It was.... The tide was half way out, or so. By dad, I stood up straight to see was there any seaweed over there at the shore and I saw the woman there, at the shore standing up, oh, she was not as far as her knees in the sea and she had a comb and she was combing her hair, combing every side. Aye, and smoothing herself and shaking herself. And by dad, it was all right. I stayed a good while looking at her while she was smoothing herself below and around herself.

By dad, a man came then. The day was then breaking and coming and the man came to me. And the kind of man he was: he couldn't see, Micilín, who was living over at Forma village. A man whom they call Little Michael, [living] over at the Forma quarter, he was not able to see [well].

'Do you see below,' said I, 'do you see the woman below,' said I, 'who is smoothing herself and combing herself?' Indeed it was as well for me to point out the fencing wall at him in order to show her [the mermaid] to him, because it wasn't clear to him, the poor man. It was not clear to him.

By dad, oh, she threw herself far out into the sea, oh, smoothing herself and washing herself. She was washing her neck and washing so that you would think that it was time for her to, be washed in the sea, if it was in the sea ... but really it was not in the sea that one was. Upon my soul [it appeared] that she had a dwelling place far out in the sea. I would say for sure that she had it there.

Furthermore he made some noise. Oh, she raised her head. This old man, he made some noise with something and oh, she lifted her head up into the air and she looked around her and with that she was gone. Out with her to the sea ... eastward with her, eastward with her and she did not go down or anything like it. But stayed on top of the sea swimming away with herself heading forward. That's all I can tell you. I don't know where her dwelling place is.

Question: But did you not think that it was an ordinary girl, that was having a swim, a girl from the island or a visitor?

Storyteller: It was not!

Question: It surely was not?

Storyteller: Oh, that was not that kind of person she was.

Question: Are you sure?

Storyteller: Oh, it wasn't. Oh, she would not be there as early as that, you understand?

Question: Would she not?

Storyteller: Oh, she would not. But I am telling you that she swam eastward and away with herself. Away she went wherever her abode was or wherever she went to. Oh, there was a skin as white as snow on her.

Question: And was she a woman all over?

Storyteller: Yes, she was a woman all over indeed, upwards from the waist on especially and higher up than that as well.

Question: And the other part of her.

Storyteller: Yes, she was completely [in the shape of] a woman. O, indeed, it is often we heard talk about the queen of the sea or the ....

— Chapter Nine —

WORK TABOOS AND OTHER WONDER STORIES

70 **Holy Water Sends the Redweed Ashore**
*Val Ó Donnchadha, Bantrach Ard,
Cill Chiaráin*

Usually, in the olden times, the people of this place, used to go to the shore. At the time, the end of night was the proper time to go gathering and bringing up redweed. For they had no other means save that redweed, spreading it out on the ground as potato fertiliser.

Because, the place where the blackweed and islands were, other people had it, big shots, I am as well to call them, who had the law in their own hands. And if any poor man or tenant went there, collecting a load of seaweed, they would prosecute him. You were as well to go anywhere — they were tyrants.

But the creatures used to be gathering the redweed and then when spring would come, they would have it spread out. And there was no talk of guano or fertiliser or anything of the sort at that time. They had it [the seaweed] divided into plots down on the shore, each person had his own, and you keep yours and leave the other man's behind you. But usually, if it was plentiful or if they were good neighbours, very often there was nothing about it, but for the first man there to gather it.

It was always said that there was no better stuff to fertilise potatoes than redweed winter fertiliser, laid out in winter. Then when spring would come, if they got the chance to get a few loads of blackweed to spread over it as second manuring and let that become fallow with the sun and rain, until it became second manuring, they would then spread their seed potatoes on it. And they used to say that there was never a better kind of fertiliser for potatoes in Connemara, as this kind of seaweed.

At any rate, it happened at the time that there wasn't the slightest bit of redweed coming ashore and no one knew the reason. But they were worried that they might not have any seaweed. My grandfather, my father's father, Pádraig Ó Donnchadha, was living in An Aird Mhór. It was supposed that the reason [that there was no seaweed] was, that people were gathering seaweed on Sunday nights and that this [lack] was meant as revenge, maybe.

He went of an evening with a bottle of holy water and started at this end of the shore and proceeded as far as the bottle lasted, a drop here and a drop there, saying his prayers and praying to God...I believe it was his good belief, saying prayers and asking God to send the seaweed in, as it used to come before [which saved the seaweed]. On the morrow, thanks be to God and the miracles of God and the holy water, the shore was full with redweed. And they remarked greatly at this and everyone was saying that He had performed a great miracle.

71 Horse Breaks Knee of May-Day Seaweed-Gatherer
Máirtín Seoighe, Baile an Fhorma, Inis Oírr

They were here one day and there was a lot of seaweed on the rocky shore. In Inis Meáin it happened. And as there was, they said, 'There is a lot of seaweed on the rocky shore,' they all said to each other, 'and by dad, we don't know what we will do with it.' 'There is a lot of seaweed on the rocky shore and even so, we don't like to straddle any horse, today, May Day.' 'Muise,' says this fellow, 'I'll straddle my horse,' says he.

This fellow brought his horse in from the enclosure out onto the yard, and he lay out the straddle and his baskets. And his horse was tied to the wall. But he threw some potatoes to the horse and she was eating them. He put the straddle up, he lay the straddle on its back. And when he did, he tied the bellyband, and he fixed up the straddle and everything and put his baskets up [on the horse]. 'I don't know,' says he, 'if the shoes ... if any of the horse's shoes are loose,' says he.

He raised her hind leg up. He looked at it and when he did, that shoe was all right. And when it was, he lifted the front leg and looked at it and it was firm. And when he went around in this manner with this leg, to see how the shoe on the other side was, she kicked him. And she knocked him flat in front of the door and broke his knee.

His wife heard him shouting outside. She went to him 'Oh, what's wrong with you?' says she. 'I am killed by the horse.' 'More luck to you,' said his wife to him, 'isn't it May Day,' said the wife to him. 'Didn't we always hear,' said she, 'that it wasn't right to straddle a horse on May Day.' 'Well, we know it today,' says he. 'My knee is broken.'

By dad, there was nothing to be done. A currach brought him to Cill Rónáin, back to the doctor and his leg was broken. He had to be sent to Galway hospital for fifteen days, and his leg was in traction, and he spent fifteen days [there]. And when it [the leg] was released after the fifteen days, it was knotted. Anyways, he came home but he said that he would never straddle a horse again on May Day.

72 The Sea Takes back the Seaweed of St Stephen's Day
Val Ó Donnchadha, Bantrach Ard, Cill Chiaráin

I remember well — it's a good number of years ago — the whole family of us was here, that time: my brothers, God rest the soul of those that are gone, and the man I was talking about, Pádraic, he is alive in America, in Chicago.

Now then, there was a man in this village of ours who was connected with us ... he was a neighbour of ours; he was closely related to us. His name was N.N.* Anyhow, he was ever so avaricious concerning the seaweed shore. He used to be searching for wreckage, searching for seaweed and so on.

Anyway on Stephen's Day morning or at the end of Saint Stephen's Day's night he came to the door, to that house beside us in which we were living that time and growing up into lads, and he woke us up. He said to Pádraic, 'Get up, Pádraic,' said he, 'and go out,' says he. 'The rocky shore is full of red seaweed, and we shall put a part of it up to the highwater mark, (and) isn't it a great sin,' says he 'to let it go out again with the tide.'

---

* N.N. is to represent the Connemara man's name.

'Oh,' says Pádraic, 'The devil I care,' says he, 'who will go down. It may go where it wants to,' says he. 'But the dickens a hand I shall lay on any sprite of seaweed,' says he, 'on the feast of blessed Stephen,' says he, 'and perhaps you would be just as thankful to yourself,' says he, 'if you would listen to that.'

But the man N.N. went down. He began to gather seaweed, but there was no gathering for him, just to throw it up as far as the strength of his hand was able to put it with the fork and you would not recognise it in the evening when he was finished that he took a fork full out of it with the amount that was there.

This is how it was and in the night the wind changed and went south-east. There was a stir in the sea and it got up as if it was the will of God. And the next morning, when the first man got up and looked down, there was not as much red seaweed on the rocky shore of Connemara as you would put into your pipe.

It was Saint Stephen who put it out again. A lesson he got (the man N.N.), a lesson. It was not right to go gathering it on Saint Stephen's feast day.

73 The Sea Takes Sunday Seaweed
Máirtín Ó Domhnaill, Baile Thiar, Inis Oírr

There was a man here in Baile an tSéipéil once, and he had no help but himself. He had young children. He needed a stack of seaweed to spread as winter manure at Christmas. The young men used to visit him. And one night he brought two of them with him. It was a Saturday night, you know, it was after midnight. And they gathered a great stack of seaweed. They were gathering for two hours. Then they went home and when they got up in the morning they hadn't a bit of the seaweed left.

The sea arose and swept away all the seaweed from them. They thought [that this happened] on account of working on Sunday, because of the ban on work. It's not right to do that.

74 Sunday's Seaweed without Crop
Labhrás Ó Conghaile, Baile an Fhorma, Inis Oírr

When I was a young boy in our own house with the family, we had a brother in the house. He used to go around with another companion and they said that the shore was full with seaweed on Sunday night. My mother and my father said not to go but he did. And they brought up the seaweed to the high ground and it was put out on the field the next day. And the amount that was brought up on the Sunday night, no potato whatsoever grew in it, only weeds. And the seaweed that was spread on the Monday morning, directly next to it, a fine crop of potatoes grew in it. That's it now. That's all there is to that. What was gathered on the holiday,* nothing grew on it.

---

* i.e. on the Sunday.

75 Instructive Revelation on Sunday Work
Labhrás agus Máirtín Ó Conghaile, Baile an Fhorma, Inis Oírr

Labhrás: It is said that the Sunday work ban is not over until you can see the small stone* and the big stone on Monday morning?

Oh, they often gathered [seaweed] here on a Sunday night. They used to say it was no harm [to gather] seaweed, but they preferred not to gather seaweed at that time. You'd like to go and have it when it would come ashore, when the tide would leave it on the shore, so that when I would come along after you, I couldn't touch it. You'd have it gathered up, below at the rocky shore.

And people used to gather it as manure. It was an instructive revelation to them. They'd spread it and no seed or anything would grow in the place where Sunday seaweed had been spread. That's true.

Máirtín: I myself gathered it one Sunday night and we spread it the next day on the field to grow potatoes. And not a single potato whatsoever grew there. And we had seaweed again on Monday and we spread that on the field and potatoes grew on that.

It was in April. They didn't grow.** And we spread the other amount of what came in with the tide on Monday and potatoes grew on it.

---

* The reference is to the small and big stones in a dry-stone wall. It is said that Sunday is not fully ended until it is bright enough to distinguish these stones from each other. Work may not be commenced until it is perfectly bright, i.e. until Monday has properly begun.

** Speaker picks up thread of thought of first idea again.

76 Christmas Seaweed Did Not Rot
Val Ó Donnchadha, Bantrach Árd,
Cill Chiaráin

Long ago when I was young, and years before ... but they did not use to do it during my time ... I don't remember the time when they used to do it, but ... the crowd that came before me, they used to say that they used to abstain from work the twelve days of Christmas, from Christmas Eve till the Feast of the Epiphany.

Anyhow, there was a man of this village here drawing red seaweed with his horse. Pádraig Ó Catháin was his name. He was living then on the other side of the road, and he was a young man at that time.

Anyhow, there was a load over ... [he had] a big load on his horse and it was very late, the night was Christmas Eve. And he was going over a drain or a dyke and the load turned over to one side, and the packsaddle and the basket and everything that was there fell. It was late and he was tired. And he threw the packsaddle off and he loosened the tying ropes and he said to himself, 'Ah, well God save us,' says he, 'I have worked sufficiently hard today and upon my word,' says he 'you may stay there till Christmas is over, even if you rot away or not.'

And he took the horse home. He put here into the stable and gave her a rest. He did not see the seaweed from Christmas Eve till the Feast of the Epiphany when he went that way.

And there was the load of seaweed, the water was underneath and on top of it, red weed which rots very easily. And, a thousand thanks to the Son of God, after the twelve days the load of seaweed was as fresh as on the day when it came in from the sea.

77 Seal as Omen of Dry Weather
Peadar Seoighe, Baile an Fhorma, Inis Oírr

One day when I was a young man and in good health, I was over at the shore. There were also two or three neighbours there, you understand. By my soul, there weren't any binoculars at that time, nor any radio. All you hear now is: '*Tá weather thoir agus an weather thiar, is blowing here and blowing there.*' That time you would have to look up at the star in the morning, at daybreak, or you would have to go out at night and look at the moon when going to bed.

One man here, he said ... he was up at our house visiting one night, Mikey they used to call him ... he looked out the door as he was going home at ten o'clock and said: 'There is a garden (i.e. a halo) round the moon tonight.'

He had a kind of friend [with him]: 'Where is the wall-gap in it?' 'Ha, ha, ha,' said Mikey, 'if I showed you the opening in the wall, you would have your donkey in there in the morning, because I think that there is fine grass altogether in that field.'

Well, when there is a halo on the moon, you understand, at the beginning of the night, they would say that you would have rain on the evening of the following day.

Anyway, I was over on the shore, this particular day, and there was a woman there, indeed, the poor creature, she was a great woman for work and a great woman for the shore. She also was a great help to her husband.

She came over with the dinner. So she brought a grand basket of bread, a fine can of tea and indeed whatever kind of tea she had the devil the likes of it you never saw. She would not have any regard for it unless it was really strong.

If the hen were to put her foot into the mug, the tea would keep her up. Indeed it would have to be very strong tea ... that it would be strong.

Anyhow, we were all working during the morning and one man began to say to the other: 'It looks like rain, I'm afraid that we will get rain tonight and there is no use putting up this seaweed, because it is not very strong.' You know, plenty of moss and messy stuff comes into some of the shores. Back out there at the lighthouse the finest of seaweed comes ashore. But we were over at Trá Caorach (Sheep Strand) on that day.

That woman herself was there. Indeed she was a great woman to fill a basket. And if she got a day filling it for you at the shore or half way up to the high-water mark over there in Trá Caorach, the devil you would rise for a week afterwards, because every basket would weigh from ten stone to half a hundredweight. It would mean having a good job done, when you would have a dozen or a score of them brought down into the enclosure.

The poor man was there and we were talking. I believe that we lit the pipe and put a grain of tobacco into it and we continued talking. We were all very satisfied when — what do you think happened — a devil of a seal came, and there was never a day that I saw a seal over in the shore that it didn't announce a dry spell of weather.

'By dad,' says a man, Keane we used to call him, 'well,' said he to the woman, 'we were just saying before that it was going to rain. The devil a day I saw the seal there on Leic an Chalaidh,' said he, 'but you would not get a week of dry weather.'

There was this man, the husband of the woman then, the poor man he had spent the whole night working, and he was very tired and overtired.

'Oh, now,' says he, 'get up and let us go down again. Michael says that the seal is on Leic an Chalaidh, that there will be a dry spell for a week.'

'Ah, well, bad luck to yourself and to the seal,' says the man.

On my soul, the devil a stop he made again until evening. He kept carrying back the baskets to the crag after that, the poor man. He was tired! And, by cripes, whether the seal knew it, or whether he didn't, or whatever way he found out, the dry spell came. However, Mary made nearly half a ton of kelp that day. Well, that's now more or less all I know about that story.

78 Seal Prevents Seaweeders from Working *
Pádraic Ó Máille, Cor na Rón Láir
Indreabhán

There** are many stories of that type about them that I heard, but I know anyhow, that it happened back in Ros a' Mhíl — back there — it's not far — that they were one day....

There used to be a lot of people gathering seaweed that time, do you know? I heard my mother — the Lord have mercy on her — describing it.

And when they went to the rocky shore gathering the seaweed, the seal was in a pool, in the pool that the tide had

---

*   There are quite a number of stories concerning seals, and their submarine habitat, in my collection, however as these do not relate directly to seaweed they have not been included.

**   On the subject of seals see, Christine Agricla, *Schottische Sagen*, Berlin: 1967, 122 an 273ff.

left. All who were going gathering seaweed saw the seal beside them in the pool. They didn't know how to go around it and they were afraid to go around it. What they did was to ask for help. Guns weren't very common that time. But they went down to the station looking for a waterguard, do you know, he was a coastguard, who used to be looking after the coasts. He used to have a gun and there were a good many of them around that time under English Rule, like, they are sort of coastguards looking after the coasts.

But he had a gun at any rate and the man came back with the lad that went down to fetch him. And he started firing at the seal and there wasn't a shot that he would fire that the seal wouldn't bend its head and let it past it.

He spent the whole time that it was ebbing firing at the seal and he didn't kill it and he didn't hit it [either].

The seal and all that were going gathering seaweed stayed there that day — it was a high-tide — all those who were going gathering seaweed didn't do anything, not a thing, but watch him firing at the seal.

When the tide reached the seal, the seal went out into the sea again and headed off with nothing done to him. There was no lie in that. People were saying that it wasn't a real seal.

79 Broken Taboo of Silence Impedes Fern Cure
Peadar Seoighe, Baile an Fhorma, Inis Oírr

At last we were ready and we began to rake. Then there were two; the two [kelp]-burners had a spade [each]. We were raking away and we had half the kiln ready and were making good progress. But at last didn't it (the kelp) burst out through the wall. The wall, it opened with the force of the heat, do you understand. But a hole came in [the wall] and out it came. And when it did, didn't it land on the burner's foot. It would burn you as badly as boiling water when it would land on you, or as if you struck your foot in the fire.

But we always had the habit, that if your foot were burnt like that and no one were to speak, if you ran back anywhere in the crag, got a bunch of ferns and applied it to the spot that was burnt, you were cured. And if the man ran back and no one there spoke the cure was effected.

However this day, the poor man didn't go, do you understand, fast enough. He didn't run. There was this stranger there. 'Oh what are you doing,' says he. 'Go off to the crag immediately,' says he, 'and get a bunch of ferns; isn't your foot...in a bad state?'

'Oh muise, may you be choked alive and kicking,' says he. 'Now it is certainly cured nicely! Indeed now there is no cure in store for me,' says he, 'since you spoke. Didn't you know?'

'Oh I am sorry about it,' says he, 'I could not help it,' said he, 'But next time I will know better,' said he. But the burner did not go back then since this man spoke. But indeed he had bad luck with his foot, because kelp could really burn you and I mean burn. But the cure would have been easy afterwards in a way because there were great healing power in the kelp.

80 Curing Skin Disease by Bladderwrack
Mícheál Ó Donnchadha, Baile Thiar, Inis Oírr

A man from Connemara was telling me that he was very bad with a skin disease. It was a kind of rash, it completely covered his skin all over. He was in the hospital in Galway. He was there a long time and they couldn't clear it. They didn't do him any good. He was a little better when he left the hospital, but it was not cleared up completely. He went home then, but he got worse than before. He came back in again to the hospital in Galway and he was a short while there. They weren't healing him. They sent him up to Dublin, to the hospital — I don't know now what the name of the hospital is — anyhow, he spent two months there, but they didn't heal him. He was a little better. They told him to go home and to come back again if he got worse.

So he came home. He heard about a woman — an old woman who lived in the place, a good distance from him — who had a cure for this but he wasn't sure of what he heard. Nevertheless, he was so bad that he went to her. What she told him was, that there is a kind of seaweed which they call bladder-wrack — you know now that black seaweed which we put out in the fields; well, there isn't much of it here, but there is plenty of it in Connemara. We usually put it out on the fields in Spring as fertiliser. Black seaweed or bladder-wrack they call it. I think bladder-wrack is the right name for it. So she told him to get that and to put it into a pot, some of it, and to boil it, to boil it well.

When the seaweed would be well boiled, and well mixed, and pressed together (I don't know what they call it in Irish) and a kind of jelly made of it, a poultice of seaweed and juice, and should be put or rubbed on the skin. In any case, he did as well as he could with it. He would do anything to get rid of this rash. So he did as best he could and he kept doing it. Inside a month there wasn't a trace on his skin no more that there was on his clothes. There really wasn't. So he was rid of it then. He would apply the seaweed now and again and hold on to the water in which it was boiled. He kept rubbing it on his skin and he was getting on very well. None of the skin disease remained. They told him in the hospital in Dublin and in Galway to have nothing to do with alcohol, which he didn't during this time.

When he had improved, like everyone, he ignored his good health. He started to take drink on a special occasion. A cousin of his got married and he was his best man and there was great merry-making going on. He took a drop and the buck (the disease) came back again; so he had to fall back on the seaweed cure. I met him again in the hospital in Galway. He was back there. He had to apply the seaweed again and it cleared the rash. That last time in there when I was talking to him he wasn't drinking and if he abstained from the drink since, I'm sure that he would be free from this blemish.

81 Sea Urchin's Spikes Can be Removed with the Ebb Tide
Peadar Seoighe, Baile an Fhorma, Inis Oírr

On this particular day I was coming home. There used to be a poor old man working on the shore and as he was there I met him. 'It would appear that you are lame,' said I. 'Oh, I am,' says he. 'The place was very slippery, and I was thrown into a rock pool of water,' says he. 'Well, indeed, my heel is in a bad state. Could you help me in any way?' 'Indeed,' said I, 'any way I can be of assistance to you, poor man.'

He was carrying a big basket of seaweed and he fell into the pool. 'But it would appear that you are very lame,' said I. 'Oh I am,' says he, 'my foot is in a bad way.' 'What happened to you?' 'Ah,' says he, 'I don't know. There are about ten or twenty spikes from a sea urchin in my heel. I have a needle here. I will sit down, and it will be as well to tackle them,' says he.

'Indeed, I will,' said I, 'with pleasure, if I am able to get them out. But as the old people used to say,' said I, 'they cannot be removed with the ebb tide.' 'I don't care, whether ebb or flow now,' says he. 'I am not able to go home, and indeed I will not sleep a wink tonight,' says he, 'unless you take them out.'

He had a needle. 'You know, of course, that there are three types of needles: there is a small needle; the old women had a needle in order to darn socks.' But indeed, this poor man had a particular big needle, nearly six inches long, fine and strong, and it had a good sharp point on it.

I myself set to work on his heel. The poor man! Indeed, I felt sorry for him. You know, if you went to take a thorn out of a child's finger, it would be screaming all the time. Or if you went to take a thorn out of someone's finger, he would have great pain.

However, I was working on his heel and I took out a few thorns that were not too far in. But in the end I was not making any headway with a particular one — it had gone in very deep. 'Oh,' said I ... 'What are you doing?' says he. 'I am doing my best,' said I. 'Well now, give me fair play! I am taking my time.'

'Ah, you rogue you,' says he, 'don't spare the flesh,' says he, 'don't spare the flesh! Work them out towards you,' says he.

Question: Would they get into your fingers also?

Answer: They would. It's often now, we would be gathering seaweed, you understand. The weed would be here, when we gathered it ... You would never think that one of them would go into the top of your finger. Well, whatever would be in your finger at ebb tide, it would go in further. The thorn itself would harden. Somehow it can't be taken out. According to the nature of the incoming tide — whatever nature that is — the thorn softens and it is easy to take it out. Oh, it is easy to take it out then. That's quite certain. It is a peculiar thing. But then there are peculiar things in the world.

82 The Secret of the Danes' Fertiliser
Labhrás Ó Conghaile, Baile an Fhorma, Inis Oírr

This* field now, when it was been planted long ago, when the Vikings had this country, they needed no fertiliser, they had the field-fertiliser at the end of the ridge. And when the crowd that expelled the Vikings from this country, came ... wait till I know ... I don't remember this fellow who came in. He fought and expelled the Vikings.

Anyhow, they were all gone except for a father and son, and this crowd who had seized the country, told the father they would let him live, if he told them where the fertiliser for each field and each meadow and so on, was.

'Well,' says he, 'I'll tell you,' says he, 'but kill my son first,' says he, 'and I'll tell you.' They killed the son and when they

---

* The story was told by Labhrás outside, in the field in question.

did, 'Here now,' says he, 'kill me also,' says he, 'and let you and all that come after me have hardship for ever.' Then they killed him.

Well, there's not a spot on the crags nor anywhere where there is a bit of clay, that they could not plant that time. They had the fertiliser, what ever sort it was, they had it. You'd still see, if you were out on those crags, little spots in the crag. They used to have them planted. It was they who had it planted, the Vikings. They were on this island. They were.

I heard from all the old people, when they were getting hardship from the fertiliser, drawing seaweed on their backs and so on, they were cursing the Vikings, who didn't reveal how the fertiliser was to be got, so that people wouldn't suffer hardship for ever. But who is this at all who was fighting them?

[Prompt]: Brian Boru.

Yes, it is, the time of Brian Boru, who defeated the Danes in the battle of Clontarf.

We were back in Seán's house the other year. And this old Dane, a 'Viking', was there, in the snug, and there were two or three children there with him also, and he stuck his head ... he's not one for the fun, that 'Viking', who's staying back in Donnchadha's house, do you know. Are you familiar with him?

Well, he was in the snug and Pádraig Ann and the gang were there and Michaeleen O'Donnell, God rest his soul, and they were talking. The other Dane was down at the lake and he was smoking in at the cliff, smoking the eels and someone said, 'It won't be long till they have the whole island [for themselves], like long ago.' 'Ah, it will be like the time of Brian Boru,' said Michaeleen O'Donnell, God rest his soul.

He [i.e. Ola] stuck his head out the door. That's your man Ola.* 'Ara, what are you talking about Brian Boru. Brian Boru lost his glass shoe.' **

83 Refuge for Tailor from Bull on Seaweed Cock
Seosamh Ó Flatharta, Baile an Chaisleáin, Inis Oírr

There was a tailor here long ago. I don't know if it was in Baile an Fhorma or in Baile an Chaisleáin that he was working. But he was working the whole day, I suppose making clothes, a waistcoat, a trousers or something.

And in the evening, when he was going home, he saw the bull heading for him. He used to be rambling the roads and everyone treated him the same, for he was provided by the government. And therefore, no one in particular took care of him.

But the tailor saw the bull coming over to Baile an Fhorma, heading towards him in a rage. The tailor had no place on earth to go. He became afraid when he saw the bull, and he had nowhere to go. But he saw a stack of seaweed built, and a ladder leaning up against its side. He just ran at full speed and headed for the ladder and up he went on top of the seaweed stack.

And when he did, the bull never stopped till he reached the stack of seaweed and he saw my man on top of the stack. The bull made for the stack with his horns and he was taking chunks out of its side, tossing the

---

*   Reference to a Danish resident of the island.
** 'Glass shoe' is for 'leasú', (fertiliser).

seaweed up in the air with his horns. And my man was up on top of the stack, holding on for his life to the seaweed, afraid that he would fall down any moment. Finally he cried out:

'Ah,' says he, 'Death is a great thing', said he, 'except guts on the horn.'

Because, he thought that when the bull would be so far in to the stack that he would thin out the stack, that the stack would collapse, and that he himself would fall down, and that the bull would just stick him with his horns. And that now is what he meant when he said 'Death is a great thing, except guts on the horn.' He'd raise him on his horns and toss him up in the air and kill him.

But as lucky as you ever saw, there was a crowd working up around the church, and as they were, they heard the commotion and noise down on the strand. And down they came and brought the dogs with them and a few sticks or something I suppose as well. And they went down and they chased the bull away from the stack. And with that the tailor was rescued.

And that's now the way I heard it. It was Tom Beag who told it to me. He lived in Baile an tSéipéil — [he was] the weaver's father.

Question: When did you hear that?

Answer: I suppose it's about twenty years ago.

84 Dogs Kill Wild Cat
Labhrás Ó Conghaile, Baile an Fhorma, Inis Oírr

What else I was looking for below in the store but seaweed, below at Poll na bPéiste one night, and I was back searching at the West Village till it was two o'clock in the night. It was a bright moonlight night. The seaweed used to come in at that time if you were manuring the fields, if you did not gather it up, you know, another man would have it.

Anyway, it would usually be taken away because we needed it for the fields below at the lake, it used to be gathered up by some neighbour every day. 'Well, indeed,' I say 'you won't get it now.'

The sea was going out. 'I shall go down now,' I said and I went ... I whistled when I was below on the dunes then, at that house below. And then I whistled ... below opposite the house of Michael Ned. I whistled and I had two dogs like this one at the house, they were outside. Anyway, they came to me and when they came they went searching for rabbits. I had great fun with them. I went down.

At any rate the seaweed was there and I began gathering it up below. There was a cliff there, a little cliff. I began to gather below. Anyway, it was nearly gathered up when I saw it going over there, like this, from rock to rock, and it had its tail straight up. Well it was so big! Oh where would you get a thing in the world that would be as big as it! Well it was as big as a big stump of a dog, as a good stump. I ran away as quick as I could and made for the cliff to be up there. And at the moment when I was up there I whistled again as well as I could. They were gone after the rabbits because the rabbits were up at night, plenty of rabbits down that way that time.

And by God my boy when the first came it did not look at me for good or bad. It moved ahead two steps towards me at that time. And when it was up on the road and inside the field it only looked to one side, to one place.

But when the other dog came — that was much stronger and much bigger. The two were hoping to push it over the top of the cliff and to push it out over the cliff into the water, into the sea. Anyway, the sea ... a northerly gale was blowing, the sea was breaking in there. The young dog went out himself straight after it.

When I saw them outside I ran as quick as I could till I got here. And when I arrived everybody was asleep. It was two o'clock or three o'clock in the night, I would say two o'clock for sure. The tea was left in the teapot by the fire. The mug, the milk, the bread and the sugar and everything was left on the table there. I ate it; I placed the chair here.

I went to the window if there weren't ... I went to the window to see ... I took and I pulled the blind of the window so that I would know if they came. The two of them were at the outside of the window on the yard and they were lying there like this. They were covered with blood and they were injured all over and their ears and their mouths injured and everything. The two of them were stretched out.

But I waited till the day came. I don't know whether he got up, whether he went down together with me. Anyhow, I don't know. But we went down in the morning and when we did the dog went down with us, this young dog. And when I went towards the place in which ... where it took it ashore it stopped and it began to look at me. I told him to go and fetch it.

It went down and it was stretched out on the storm beach, lying on its back with its feet in the air. Every tooth on that lad, four of them, was protruding from the jaws. It had a huge bright crooklike claw in its tail, as big as any hook you would see ... for pollock, or for anything. It was dead and its mouth open. The dog had killed it.

Nobody had ever seen such a cat. I made a hole in the beach, where it was deep. I got sea-rods, twisted them in its fur, and dragged it behind me. I put it in the hole and covered it with shingle.

Well, when Pat Liam came, when he heard about it, I had to go down to show him the place and he dug it up to see it. 'Ah,' he said, 'that is the fellow that I met. That is the same fellow.' But he killed Pat's dogs. None of these things exist now. But this is no lie. On my own....

Whatever kind of cat it was ... I don't know if it belonged to the sea or the land. But it had the shape of a cat ... its head was a big as a small basin. The kettle was not nearly as big as its head, that small kettle over there. It wasn't nearly ... like its head. It was black and grey and had a white spot. But the colour was grey. He took the road to the West Village and I came back this side. Pat was home before I arrived, I never went searching for wrack again. He came back around this way until he reached Johnny Tom Andy's house, from there, back to this village.

85 Bream: Half Fish, Half Seaweed
Ciarán Mac an Iomaire

One morning I went to the shore cutting black seaweed and when I had the boat ready for the seaweed a snow shower started. It was in the month of February. I went for shelter under a cliff that was near the lower part of the shore. I was sitting down at the bottom of the cliff, when I saw a long tuft of seaweed spread out on the mire. I stretched out my hand and I pulled in this tuft. It was growing out of an old shoe. I was examining the way it was growing, and saw a small fish attached to the seaweed. A part of it was fish and part of it seaweed. Back in the place where the tail should be was seaweed and all of the rest was a fish. The kind of fish it was is called rockfish. I told a lot of people about it and it would seem that they did not believe it. I do not know why such a thing should happen.

Well, in my opinion ... yes in my opinion ... I was telling the priest about this and he would not believe it right, you know. He did not think that such a thing could happen. I myself think that it happens, because the rockfish is the kind of fish that lays its eggs in the cracks of the rocks. It puts some moss over them and keeps lying on them for about three or four weeks. Maybe that a bad night came or a bad day of storm or a stir in the sea that dispersed and scattered the spawn or the eggs out of the crack or out of the nest and that they fastened themselves to the seaweed and thus got their shape. Well, if it didn't happen this way, I couldn't say anything else about it.

86 The Islanders' Way of Living
Poem by Mícheál Ó Meachair,
Baile an Chaisleáin, Inis Oírr

One of our priests wrote that our priest was used to ask help for his people whenever the government refused it. I wrote this account in case it may be thought that we are at fault.

It is three years since I wrote the lines about the hardship, the distress and toiling of the people. When the weather was better fish were plentiful; now the fish that are not stolen are caught and chased away by the foreign ships.

The poor island of Aran lies in the noble land of Ireland. It is bare, shelterless; I don't lie. Were it not for God's graces, bestowed on them by God, it were a wonder that those people manage to survive.

The people are accustomed to work continuously from November to St. Brigid's Day, breaking and smashing the rock from the time the sun rises until it goes down.

Gaps will be filled in preparing this land, rock and hillocks displaced; a lining of fine stones will be spread on it and covered with sand from the beach.

It will be fertilised by seaweed; one, or two or three coverings. Then it will be divided into narrow ridges and the seed will be sown in the earth.

Isn't it hard for these people to go bad mornings with picks, and sledge-hammers and crow-bars; wearing sheep-skins to protect their chests and untanned leather on their feet.

When storms and gale come the sand will be blown and the flat stones denuded by the bitter cold and dryness of March.

But that is not all, the case is worse than that for the poor friendly labourer of Árainn; the great summer heat withers the potato sets and dispels hope.

It is no wonder for a priest who sees his people starving to send his cap around, to seek charity from Antrim as far as the fine city of Cork.

From the beginning of Spring the men are on the waves, catching cod and ling; the women and children have to gather seaweed and fertilise the potatoes with it.

They hunt dogfish, spotted dogfish, ray and sander every day except on Sundays; they send halibut, turbot, gurnard and conger eel quickly to England.

The hunt is on for the mackerel from St Patrick's Day on; from Casla to Kerry's Mount Brandon; the big ships sail east from the Scairde and the currachs north from Hag's Head.

When it is caught first its meat is too expensive for the poor man for his meal; it will be sent over [to England] in the grasp of the yellow man as it can't be bought in Ireland.

There are more kinds of fish in the sea than I can mention, that go there alive and dead; the piper and cow, the blenny, the shark and the seal from Kinvara, the hake, the coal-fish; the whiting and the pollock; the haddock and flat-fish — I don't lie — the lobster, the crab, the gurnard and the cuttle-fish and the salmon from the upper reaches of Lough Erne. The rockfish and the whiting will come there — everything in its own season; strapwrack to be cut and stacked there to make kelp for Ned Bán or Hazel.

There is not much to harvest there because oats do not grow in the soil; yet the landlord comes twice yearly, demanding his rent in spite of that.

The county council in Galway keenly collects its rates; but it won't build a road or a pier for them so that boats can land.

I hope now that the way the fishermen in Árainn live is understood; and that He who directs the moon has the power to calm the storms and gales.

I don't want our own true priest, Father White, to be blamed; often he was placed in mortal danger attending to the needs of the islanders.

Long life to those people who sent help to him when we were in dire straits; may they truly see the bright King of Glory above in Heaven.